# From Queer To Christ

by

## George Carneal

Library of Congress Registration Number: TXu 1-997-439

FIRST EDITION

ISBN-13: 978-0692768396
ISBN-10: 0692768394

To my Heavenly Father, words can't express my gratitude for not giving up on me when I was in darkness.

To my Lord and Savior, Jesus Christ, thank you for the priceless gift of salvation.

I want to thank my family and friends for their support during the writing of this book.

Dedicated in memory of my sister, Gina, and grandmother, Ella Mae Stanley.

# Table of Contents:

# 1. Introduction

For years I struggled with my Christian faith *and* homosexuality. Raised in the South (the Bible Belt) by a father who was a Southern Baptist minister, I want to share my painful journey through a secular world at odds with homosexuality and a religious world that is hostile to homosexuals. Perhaps sharing the journey through the eyes, and mind, of a confused child dealing with homosexuality will give some insight into the pain and difficulty of navigating these two worlds.

I eventually spent approximately 25 years immersed in the world of homosexuality and will briefly share the pitfalls of that life. My story is not about glamorizing a life I once lived nor is it about self-pity. I am well aware that millions of people are suffering in this world for various reasons; some so horrific I dare not seek pity in any way.

This is not an attack on, nor am I a spokesperson for, the LGBT (Lesbian/Gay/Bisexual/Transgender) or Christian communities and my story is not a representation of what all LGBT individuals experience. This is merely my journey and what I learned along the way.

I share it with you for His glory, not mine.

Thank you for reading.

# 2. Springtime in Paris

Born into a Christian home in 1964, my father was a pastor and my mother was a homemaker. When I was six years old, my father would be called to pastor a church in Paris, Tennessee.

My tall, muscular father proudly wore his Elvis sideburns. My father has a great sense of humor but also a serious side, especially when it's concerning preaching God's word. He never hesitated to call out any kid moving or talking too much in church. To him, every lost soul was a battle to be won for the Lord and a distraction of any kind was Satan's way of keeping that lost soul from being saved. I grew up hearing the real hellfire and brimstone sermons. You were aware of what sin was and the seriousness of it.

Being from the South, in what some call "the land of big hair," my short, five-foot, two-inch mother made up for her height by teasing what little frosted blonde hair she had to an unbelievable height that rounded her head and flipped out on each side. It looked like a hair-shaped bell on her head. Enough Aqua Net was used to ensure that no spring tornado could topple it.

While Tammy Wynette was singing about her "D-I-V-O-R-C-E," my mother stayed busy helping others who were less fortunate. This included befriending a woman who may have had some mental health issues and seemed unable to really care for her baby girl. However, my mother gained her trust and helped out by often bringing the infant girl home and I watched as she put her in the kitchen sink to bathe her.

After pulling numerous ticks off of her infested head, she would wash her hair. And these weren't tiny, black ticks. These were the large ones that, once squashed, would ooze blood. After the bath, my mother would put the little girl in some clean clothes and eventually return the infant to her mother.

I was the oldest of four siblings, followed by two brothers and a sister. My family dutifully attended church every Sunday morning, Sunday night, and Wednesday night.

One sweltering hot and humid day my mother sent me outside to play with my brothers. We had our cheap, plastic cups with the built-in straws filled with "sweet tea" (a treat we Southerners enjoy as much as fried food) to keep us cool while playing outside. My mother had been babysitting another infant girl. When the mother came to pick up her child I ran to the door because I was hot and thirsty. To my surprise, my thoughtful mother had already replenished my cup with more tea. Little did I know, while gulping down the beverage, that it was gasoline.

My genius brothers decided to pour gasoline into my cup as a neighbor was mowing our lawn and his gas container was nearby. I screamed and cried as I ran into the house. My insides were burning and my mother had me over the toilet while vomiting. After purging the gasoline, my throat was raw and my stomach was in pain from all the vomiting. I asked my mother for some water. She had the brilliant idea of bringing me a cold soda.

The carbonation from the soda was like drinking the gasoline all over again. It burned as it traveled down my throat. I was in misery.

I eventually started first grade and was very shy as a kid. I enjoyed reading because it allowed me to escape into another world. I developed a crush on a blonde-haired girl and a brown-haired boy in my class. While the world around me was comprised of traditional male-female relationships, I didn't understand why I had a crush on a boy as well.

Around the age of seven I felt led to give my life to Jesus. After church one night, while riding home in the back of our Volkswagen, I told my parents I wanted to be *saved*.

For those unfamiliar with what it means to be "saved," in Christianity one believes they are a sinner, and God sent His Son, Jesus, to die on the Cross for our sins. It is the *free gift* of salvation God offers to anyone who, by faith, puts their trust in Christ. After accepting Christ as your Savior, you would be baptized.

"Baptism" is symbolic. You are saying to the world that you identify yourself as a follower of Christ. Being submerged in water represents the death and burial of Jesus (symbolizing we are no longer slaves to self or sin). Rising out of the water represents the resurrection of Jesus (symbolizing our being raised to a new life in Christ, born into the family of God, and promised eternal life with our Lord and Savior, Jesus Christ).

The following Sunday I nervously walked to the front of the church where my father was waiting and made my profession of faith before the church. I had given my life to Jesus. My father would eventually baptize me.

We weren't in Paris very long as in my fourth grade year my father resigned from the church. I was too young to comprehend that problems in the church would be the norm. There would be members who were there for the wrong reasons, had ulterior motives, wanted to control the pastor, dictate how things were to be done in the church, or perhaps they just didn't like my father. My father wasn't perfect but he certainly had his own thoughts about how things should be done and stuck to his guns. At the end of the day it was about getting people into church and "saving lost souls."

During the transition period until my father found a new church, we briefly moved to a different part of town. I attended a small school that resembled something you would see on *Little House on the Prairie*, but slightly larger with a second floor. Being shy, moving to a new location and having to meet new people was very stressful.

I soon had a bully to contend with who made every effort to catch me after school and taunt me. I caught on early how to be aware of my surroundings in order to avoid the bullies. One time this kid caught up with me as I made a quick dash out the front door of the school, trying to blend in and hide behind other kids. He didn't punch me but followed me all the way home while spewing his venom at me. I said nothing and walked as fast as I could to get home.

One afternoon, when dinner was ready, my mother told me to go find my brothers. I walked around the neighborhood yelling their names without any luck. I decided to check the wooded area behind the school. As I made my way down a dirt path, deep into the woods, across the stream of water and up the other side of a steep embankment, I eventually came to a clearing. What I saw startled me.

I saw a long row of houses that looked more like dilapidated shacks. They were painted with bright colors and set against a backdrop of a blue sky that mingled with the brown smog from the factories. I saw two "colored girls" walking, one with a red afro and large hoop earrings. I gathered this was what many white folks were referring to when they spoke of "colored town." I quickly ran through the woods and back to my house. It was strange to discover two different worlds separated by trees. I had never seen anything like it. The South was very segregated at the time and I only remember one black kid in my first grade class.

# 3. Shelbyville

When my father assumed the pastorate at a church in Shelbyville, Tennessee, it meant I'd be attending the third school during my fourth grade year. I was terrified at the thought of facing yet another new, unknown place.

It was the early '70's, a time of hula hoops, lava lamps, skate boards, colorful bell-bottom fashions, *The Brady Bunch*, roller disco at the skating rink, and drive-in movies. I enjoyed album releases from the latest bands that had exotic artwork with lyrics included so you could follow or sing along with the music.

In the sleepy, middle-class suburb where I grew up, most families attended church. Sometimes churches would hold weeklong revivals. This was where a visiting pastor would come and stir up your passion for the Lord and desire to win lost souls to Jesus! Most children obeyed their parents and you were taught to show respect to your elders. Manners were expected. "Yes, sir," "No, ma'am," "Please," and "Thank You" were common words in our vocabulary.

My summers were spent fishing, riding my bike, playing in the woods and spending long days at the pool with my brothers to beat the heat. As Van Halen loudly "Danced The Night Away" over the jukebox, we did cannonballs off the side of the pool. We focused our attention on ladies on rafts who wouldn't completely submerge themselves in water to keep from getting their freshly coiffed hairdo's wet. We made sure their hair was in shambles by the time we finished bombarding them with water.

One time my brothers found a pair of used men's underwear on the locker room floor. They dragged me into the locker room, stuffed the wet underwear on my head, then pushed me back out into the public pool area where everyone could see. It was disgusting, and humiliating, but I have to admit it was comical because we did stuff like that to each other all the time.

When my father would take us to the skating rink, we had fun chasing one another while stopping long enough to do the hokey pokey when the announcer was ready. Sometimes I would just skate around the rink, in a trance, being "Blinded by the Light" as Manfred Mann sang. I lost myself in the music while watching the disco ball in the center of the rink as the colored lights danced around the room. To me, it was magical!

Because my father's church salary didn't pay enough to raise a family of six, my mother would cut our hair to save money. No, she didn't have a cosmetology license. She inflicted her hair horrors upon me, and my siblings. I honestly think she envisioned an imaginary bowl on our heads and we all ended up looking like Moe from *The Three Stooges* but with uneven bangs.

Every Tuesday was "visitation night" where a group of men would go out into the community and invite people to our church and share the Gospel with those who didn't know about Jesus. I enjoyed accompanying my father on occasion and remember one particular evening that certainly had an impact on me.

We visited the home of an elderly man who was an alcoholic. While my father was in the back room, cleaning up vomit and trying to help the man, I sat at the kitchen table. The stench of alcohol and vomit was heavy in the air. I glanced around the dimly lit room and tried to keep my feet off the floor as they kept sticking to the linoleum. I couldn't help but wonder if it was because of spilled alcohol or vomit. I was probably around nine or ten years old at the time. I'll never know if the gentleman ever came to know the Lord but my father explained how alcohol had destroyed the lives of many people, and I listened.

When the single, "Puppy Love," hit the airwaves, I fell in love with Donny Osmond. My parents purchased Donny's album, *Too Young*, and gave it to me for Christmas. It was purple with a photo of Donny on the cover. I thought he was incredibly handsome and kissed the cover a few times.

One summer, Donny Osmond was a guest on *The Merv Griffin Show*. Donny appeared in the audience, the girls screamed and swooned, and he gave one lucky girl a flower and sang to her. I was envious of the girl but kept my feelings in check for fear my excitement over a guy would cause my mom to think I was weird.

When it was announced The Osmonds would be in concert in Nashville, I asked my parents if I could go. I was told, "No, rock music is of the devil." Who knew the squeaky clean Osmonds were being used by Satan. Thankfully, my next-door neighbor attended the concert and was kind enough to give me some of the memorabilia she purchased.

When I wasn't swooning for Donny, I was busy putting together a jigsaw puzzle of Farrah Fawcett based on the best-selling poster where she wore a red one-piece swimsuit. While straight boys around me lusted after her, I focused on that hair. What hair she had! I even used the Farrah Fawcett shampoo because I thought it would give me hair like hers. On Wednesday nights I couldn't wait to get home from church in time to watch *Charlie's Angels*.

When I entered fourth grade at the new school it wasn't long before the bullying and name-calling began. Other kids would call me "sissy," "queer," "queer bait," and "faggot." It was humiliating. In the looks department I was awkward, short, awfully skinny, had big pointed ears, buck teeth, and a tacky haircut, courtesy of my mother. Kids would make fun of me but I did my best not to break down in front of them and cry.

In addition to being ostracized by the boys, probably because I was shy and effeminate, recess was another reminder of how I would never fit in with them. When the captains would choose teams, I was usually picked last. It hurt because I knew they weren't really "choosing" me, they were simply "stuck" with me. I hated sports because I feared being physically hurt. I didn't mind kickball because all you had to do was kick a ball and run. I preferred to hang out with the girls and jump rope or play "Jacks."

"Red Rover" was another game we often played. It involved two teams divided into two rows that faced each other and called out, "Red Rover, Red Rover, send (a kid's name) on over!" When your name was called, you had to run as fast as you could and break through the entwined arms of two people on the other team. If you succeeded, you could take a person back to your team. If you failed, you were now on their team. The team with the most people at the end won the game.

One time, in the middle of a game, the gym teacher appeared and told us recess was over. One of the many bullies pulled me aside and informed me that he and some other boys had planned to call my name and when I ran over to them they were going to hurt me. I stood there in stunned silence. I'm not even sure why he chose to share that information, but it frightened me.

During my fourth grade year, one bully walked up to me, called me a "sissy," and punched me in the face as I was walking to my next class. I ran crying to the principal's office and had a black eye for several days.

In my early teens, a much older bully approached me in the lunch line at school. He got directly in my face, gave me a stone-cold look, and calmly said he was going to slit my throat. I didn't even know the guy and was confused as to why he hated me so much. Fortunately, I never saw him again. I was always filled with anxiety at school. I never felt safe or had anyone who looked out for me.

My father would sometimes drive a school bus to make ends meet. I was surprised one afternoon when I climbed aboard the bus to see my dad in the driver's seat. I said "hello" and made my way to a seat.

Another bully started thumping me on the ear and calling me a sissy. When I looked in the direction of my father, I noticed he was watching the bully through the rear-view mirror. My father quickly arose from his seat, approached the guy, and sternly told him he had better sit down. I couldn't help but wonder if my father heard the bully calling me a sissy. I was humiliated by the whole incident.

The bullying was constant and I learned to accept it. I even got teased about the way I walked and carried my books. The boys carried them on the side of their hip but I carried them close to my chest, the way girls carried them. I wasn't aware of it or the way I walked until the boys teased me about it.

School was really the beginning of feelings of self-hatred and inferiority. I was always stressed out and looking over my shoulder for bullies while trying to make sure I didn't carry my books like a girl or "swish" when I walked. School wasn't about learning. For me, it was about survival.

I threw myself into areas of school where I felt at ease and could excel including art, band, and chorus. I enjoyed being creative, singing, and playing the alto saxophone.

My brothers spent their free time playing with the other neighborhood kids but I spent my time alone in my room, lost in the music of the Bee Gees, Donna Summer, Eddie Money, Elton John, Genesis, Rod Stewart, and various other artists. Music was my escape.

I would put a t-shirt on my head and pretend it was hair while taking several socks and pretending they were pom-poms. In my mind I was a popular, pretty cheerleader and pretended I had a boyfriend. As Rare Earth played on the radio, telling me to "Get Ready," I did! Emulating the same moves as the cheerleaders at school, I made up my own cheer routines, kicking a leg high up in the air while "shaking my groove thing." Peaches & Herb would have been proud. In spite of this, I was very lonely. Dreaming of having a boyfriend was my way of escaping the pain of loneliness.

I showed interest in girls to fit in with other boys. I invited a girl to a church-sanctioned hayride and we kissed underneath the blanket. She also left a big purple hickey on my neck. I was so scared my parents would see it that I spent the next few days wearing turtleneck sweaters. I had no idea what their reaction might be and didn't want to find out.

I dated a few girls but they would eventually break up with me because I was too shy and nervous to make a move. Finally, I decided I wasn't going to subject myself to that kind of rejection again. I didn't want to be with a girl to begin with. My attraction was toward boys but I didn't understand why.

When I was around nine years of age, I befriended a boy in my neighborhood. His mother invited me over to spend the night. Before bed, we took a bath together and this was my first experience with another boy. I didn't think about it being "gay." I wasn't even aware of what homosexuality was or what it meant. To me, it was a natural curiosity about the human body and we both just happened to be of the same sex. There was an interesting comfort level between us. As an adult, I learned he was also gay. Over the next few years, our explorations became more frequent as our bodies changed and I tried to understand my feelings.

High school proved to be more intimidating than middle school, especially in the locker room for gym class. I would see guys walking around showing off their muscles and hairy chests. Some of the teens were already shaving but I had very little body hair and was a late bloomer in terms of puberty so I felt even weirder. I was ashamed of my body and felt uneasy changing into my gym shorts in front of other guys. I would find a corner, quickly change, and exit the locker room.

The South, in the '70's, was also a time of unspoken animosity and hatred between many blacks and whites. Even the churches were segregated. When I was in high school, an African-American female was elected homecoming queen. The night of the homecoming game a large number of the Ku Klux Klan showed up in their robes. I quickly left the scene. The Klan's presence frightened me.

I didn't have the same racial issues many in the South had because the black girls at school treated me better than most of the white kids. For me, people were put into one of two categories: nice or bullies.

When I was 14, my father needed to go to Chicago and took me with him. It was winter, brutally cold, and the very strong winds cut through me as I walked the streets with one of the men my father was visiting. Still, the trip was amazing because the "big city experience" was exciting. I felt grown up visiting a city that was so different from small-town life in Tennessee.

We visited a church and the Sunday School class I attended had only boys in it. This was 1979, not long after serial killer, John Wayne Gacy, had been arrested for sexually assaulting and murdering at least 33 teenage boys and young men. Some of the boys called me a sissy and made crude comments about how John Wayne Gacy would have liked me. I sat there in confused silence.

How could the boys in Chicago, and the boys where I lived, make assumptions about my sexual orientation when I didn't understand my feelings or what they meant? It took quite a bit of time for me to even understand what the words "queer" and "faggot" meant. When I finally understood, I hadn't yet come to terms with the fact that I might actually be gay. I knew I was attracted to guys but didn't know why. How did *they* know? All of this was very confusing to me.

# 4. Estill Springs

During my sophomore year of high school, my father was called to minister at another church in the small, sleepy town of Estill Springs, Tennessee. It had one red light, and plenty of boredom. Again, this was scary yet exciting. It was scary because it meant a new school, new kids, and the fear of the unknown. However, almost seven years in Shelbyville had me feeling like Miss Sofia in *The Color Purple*: "I's feelin' real down. I's feelin' mighty bad." I welcomed a new start.

The middle-class suburb we moved to was near the lake. While I spent my summers swimming and tanning, the Go-Go's wanted a "Vacation," Boy George shocked the world with his androgynous appearance, and New Wave music was all the rage. Square Pegs, The Love Boat, and Solid Gold were three of my favorite television shows.

One night, not long after our move, I was outside when I saw an orange glow rising in the air. Being curious, I walked in that direction toward the train tracks. Crossing the tracks, I saw a small valley below. During the day you would normally see plenty of green grass, a forest of trees, and off to the right would be a park. On this particular night I saw three huge burning crosses and a large number of Klan members, fully robed.

The sight was terrifying and I quickly ran home. In hindsight, I wish I had stayed to watch what it was they did at those rallies. There were many days when I saw Klan members standing at the traffic intersection in their white robes and hats collecting money and passing out the Klan newspaper. Again, I didn't understand hatred toward a group of people because of their skin color.

During high school, I was curiously intrigued by two African-American publications known as *Ebony* and *Jet*. I was fascinated with black culture but feared being tormented by racist white kids, or racist black kids who might give me the stink eye, so I would strategically place books around my very large *Ebony* magazine to read it. *Jet* magazine (a smaller publication similar to *TV Guide*) could easily be placed inside a book. I would lean back like I was reading one of my school books only to be immersed in the world of black culture, the latest news, Fashion Fair cosmetics, and their "beauty of the week" which revealed a lady, her likes, measurements and Zodiac sign.

Because my father disapproved of secular music, I would secretly watch *Soul Train* whenever possible. I loved looking at the dancers' fashions when they formed the Soul Train line and did their moves. There seemed to be a unity among the young men and women who danced, smiled, and interacted in a way that seemed to embody "peace, love, and soul."

When it was time to attend my new school, I was terrified. Since the new kids didn't know the "old" me, I was determined to learn from my past mistakes, change my behavior, do things differently and, hopefully, be liked.

Most kids were drinking, smoking, and doing drugs. I started to drink beer and even experimented with marijuana because I wanted to fit in. My father's lectures on alcohol had fallen on deaf ears. I also started skipping school with two girls I went to church with. I was fed up with being bullied and being an outsider. One of them also taught me how to drive her car on the backcountry roads. When I turned 16 and secured my driver's license, I had an extra measure of freedom!

I found a job bagging groceries at a local grocery store and developed a major crush on one guy I worked with. Sometimes, in the back storage area of the grocery store, he would spend time talking to me not realizing I had a huge crush on him. Several co-workers would take turns hosting parties. It didn't take long for me to end up drunk and passed out on a bed until I slept it off.

Finally, it was the summer of '82 and graduation day arrived. I managed to get to this point without too much of the usual bullying I endured in Shelbyville but still got "fag" comments tossed my way quite often. Once the graduation ceremony was over and students threw their caps in the air with excitement, I quickly exited the football field to find my family and never looked back. I didn't stay to mingle with fellow classmates or reminisce about the "precious memories" of years gone by. School wasn't a happy place for me. As far as I was concerned, it was a prison. I had served my time and was now free.

I was finally out of high school and planned on attending a local college in the fall. While Patrice Rushen was singing "Forget

Me Not" on the radio, one afternoon I made my way to a mall in a nearby town and entered an arcade to play some video games. As I watched, a guy with dark hair played a favorite video game of mine. I couldn't help notice how attractive he was with a lean body and a hairy chest. He finished the game, we exchanged smiles, and he left.

Trying to overcome my shyness, I boldly followed him to the parking lot and watched him climb into his red Mustang. I got into my car and followed him for a bit before he noticed, pulled into a school parking lot, and stopped.

I exited my car trying to think of a good story (okay, a lie) to tell him. Thinking I was slick, I said,

"Hi, I'm sorry for following you but I lost some money at the video arcade and wanted to know if you had found it."

"No," he said.

"Oh. Okay then," I replied. I nervously stood there in silence as we smiled at each other. He must have sensed my shyness and broke the awkwardness by asking,

"Hey, would you like to have dinner with me some time?"

I excitedly said, "Yes!"

We exchanged names and phone numbers. I wasn't sure if he was gay or not but I looked forward to having dinner with him.

I didn't know what to expect when I eventually met up with Seth. I met him at his home and we discussed music while he poured over a few albums, including one of his favorite bands, Adam & The Ants. We eventually got into his car and as he drove, the conversation turned from small talk to him asking me if I was gay.

It was the first time someone had asked versus calling me a "faggot." It also was the first time that I had really been confronted with having to answer that question for myself. I looked out the passenger-side window on that sunny afternoon and hesitantly said to him, "Yes, I guess I am." He confirmed he was as well. My head was spinning with so many thoughts. We had dinner at a local restaurant and then he drove to a deserted place in the woods where we kissed for a long time.

For weeks we would hang out. I was developing feelings for him, couldn't eat, lost a lot of weight, and had knots in my stomach every time I thought of him. I had never experienced feelings like this before.

Not long into our summer "romance," he informed me he would be heading off to college in another city. I almost cried in front of him. Thankfully, I wouldn't have to know the pain of a separation because my father, who was dealing with issues at this latest church, was about to move our family. Again.

While I wasn't privy to all the details, it seemed to involve typical church politics and disagreements on how the church should operate. A Wednesday night meeting was announced in order to decide the fate of my father's ministry and the church was packed. The majority voted against my father and he resigned.

I walked outside to an isolated area of the parking lot to process what had happened. I looked up at the sky, toward the moon, and verbally stated to God, out loud, that I hated Him! Why would these "Christians" do this to my dad? Maybe it was personal to me because of my own issues of having been rejected by my peers at school, and bullied. To me, this felt like another form of bullying. I didn't know how to separate the two.

From that moment on I did everything I could to stay out of church. I had also started attending a local college and hated it. I was just going through the motions trying to please my parents. And, judging by the world around me, it appeared life was already being defined for us. Meaning, in my world, there was a well-defined path. You went to church, to school, graduated, went to college or found a job, got married, had kids, accepted whatever life handed you, and then you died. I knew there *had* to be something more to life than that and I was determined to find it.

# 5. The Sunshine State

Not long after my father resigned, he told us we would be moving to Cocoa, Florida, where God was calling him to preach at another church. I was thrilled! A new state, a new start, and we would be close to the beach! And the best part was that I didn't have to worry about another school. I was actually excited about this move. Florida was certainly different from Tennessee. Plenty of palm trees, orange trees, sunshine, and abusive humidity.

Missing Persons was one of my favorite bands at the time. I had a crush on Limahl (lead singer of Kajagoogoo). Def Leppard went on and on about a "photograph" while Duran Duran sang about some "girls on film."

We were welcomed at the new church and a fellow church member helped me find a job at a local grocery store. On my days off, when it was too cold for the beach, I would go to the mall on Merritt Island and spend most of the day playing video games since I didn't have friends yet and was bored.

One day, a blond-haired guy got my attention and invited me back to his car. We made small talk and during the course of our conversation his motive became clear. After the sex act was completed, we parted ways.

When I wasn't working, I would spend nights cruising the A1A strip along the beach, mesmerized by the lights of the clubs and hotels. I hadn't seen anything like that before in "small town" Tennessee. During the day there would be swarms of people, especially tourists, on the beaches along with tanned surfers riding the waves and sometimes dolphins swimming nearby. I also noticed a few *adult* bookstores and was curious about what those were.

On my way to the beach one morning, I stopped at one of the adult bookstores to check it out. While I nervously "cased" the joint, the store held an assortment of straight and gay porn magazines, sex toys, etc., while the back area was filled with private booths with doors that would lock. In those booths you could watch an assortment of straight/gay porn. I didn't realize the booths also had large holes in the walls to connect with other men and have sex. I quickly became addicted to this new rush of sexual pleasure.

I begrudgingly continued to attend church. One Sunday night I decided to sneak out of the service with a girl who wanted to visit her boyfriend. She was fifteen years old and unable to drive. As she visited her boyfriend, I sat in my mother's car listening to Robert Plant's song, "Big Log," playing on the radio. The girl returned to the car with a hickey on her neck. I quickly drove back to the church only to have a drunk driver plow into the passenger side of my mother's car, throwing us directly into oncoming traffic. Thankfully, the traffic was far enough away in which I had enough time to swerve back into my lane. The inebriated man attempted to blame me but, thankfully, a police officer was sitting nearby and witnessed the whole incident.

Returning to the church long after the service ended, both sets of parents were waiting for us. We explained what happened. Her parents were furious and left. My mother yelled about her car and my father threw his two cents in the mix. I was so stunned by what had happened I just listened as they ranted. I later reminded my mother that all she cared about was her precious car, never-mind that I could have been killed. When all else fails, use guilt.

Out driving one night, I saw another adult bookstore and this one was located on the A1A strip so I decided to check it out. Prostitutes congregated on the corner as I parked the car and nervously entered the establishment. Its layout was similar to the other adult bookstore and I visited both stores on numerous occasions.

Once inside, I cruised by a dark-haired guy and eventually made contact with him in a connecting booth. After the sex act, we walked outside and had a friendly conversation. Kurt and I decided to stay in touch, exchanged phone numbers, hung out often, and a real friendship ensued.

Kurt had heard about a gay bar in Cocoa Beach so we decided to check it out one night. I was 18 years old and it would be my first time in a gay bar. I felt an overwhelming mix of nervousness and excitement. Walking in, the small club was dimly lit. The bar was on the left with the dance floor to the right. In the back were pool tables and the main area had tables for men to sit and chat. I still remember the smell, the cool air, and you could smoke. I had experimented with pot and alcohol, and also started smoking. I ordered a beer and quickly finished it off while nervously fidgeting with a cigarette. I couldn't get over all of the attractive guys. They weren't the usual stereotypes you see in the media. Many of them were masculine and I wanted to be with them. I was like a kid in a candy store.

Blaring disco and dance music pulsated through the large speakers. Shannon said, "Let The Music Play" and the DJ's complied. The "Flashdance" soundtrack was riding high on the charts while The Weather Girls warned it was "raining men." While some men danced, others stood while sipping on their drinks, some played pool, some remained on bar stools in conversations with others, or cruised guys. Kurt and I sat on the barstools for a long time. I was busy taking it all in.

From that point on, I visited the bar as often as I could. I was so starved for affection that I welcomed any attention from a guy. It took some adjusting because now the attention from guys wasn't negative like it had been at school. At that time I couldn't see that it wasn't the right kind of attention I needed. Their intentions were usually for sex only but hindsight is 20/20. I was tired of being lonely *and* I wasn't being bullied. That's all that mattered.

One night, on my way to the restroom, two guys stopped me and asked if I would like to do some "coke." I had never done cocaine before and, wanting to fit in, said, "Sure." We walked into the restroom, locked the door and snorted the drug. Unlike other drugs I would eventually experiment with, cocaine didn't depress me or make me feel out of control.  It actually helped me to relax and feel more confident, especially when dancing and talking to guys.  All of the inner inhibitions seemed to disappear.  It would become my drug of choice.

Living in Florida in the early '80's, most everyone I knew in the club scene was doing cocaine.  I couldn't afford it but people kindly shared it.  If cocaine wasn't available, there was the popular amyl nitrite a.k.a. "poppers."  The little brown bottle of liquid was a cheap way to experience euphoria while temporarily freeing me of all insecurities and inhibitions.

Kurt called to say he had met a popular drag queen who invited him back to his house for the weekend and I was eventually introduced to him.

In the gay community, drag queens are like celebrities.  For those unfamiliar with that term, a drag queen is a man dressed like a woman, a female impersonator, and usually over-the-top in their appearance with dramatic make-up and huge wigs.  They usually lip-sync to a song and entertain a crowd.

In or out of drag, I found Sam to be caustic and sarcastic with a great wit and we quickly hit it off.  At the bar where he performed in drag, one night a week was designated as "strip night" and a few guys would volunteer and strip to the music.  One night, Sam decided I was going to strip.  I struggled with him as he dragged me onto the floor while my friends cheered me on.  Fine.  All alone, with the lights blinding me, I decided to block everything out of my mind and just concentrate on the beat as I danced and stripped to the music. By now, I already had enough alcohol and cocaine in me to just "let go." The music ended. I grabbed my clothes and exited the floor. I immediately walked to the bar to get another drink. I couldn't believe I had just stripped in front of a crowd of men.

I eventually met a guy that I was attracted to and we started dating. Jake lived in a guesthouse on a large estate. I enjoyed staying over and falling asleep in his arms. Unfortunately, he had a drug habit and enjoyed shooting up, especially the liquid form of Valium. He wanted me to get high with him but I was terrified of needles.

One night, as he sat on the couch, I straddled his legs and nervously watched as I waited for him to wrap a rubber tourniquet around my arm, find a vein, and insert the needle. I stared in the other direction as the drug entered my vein. The immediate rush didn't last long. I found no particular joy in that form of getting high and decided the experience fell under the "Stupid Things You Do When You're in Love" category. After several weeks, I decided to break things off and move on.

Halloween was upon us and Sam had an interesting idea. There was a bar playing the movie, *The Rocky Horror Picture Show.* The film is about a transvestite (cross-dresser) and other odd characters. Sam felt we should dress up and attend. While most attendees dressed as various characters from the movie, Sam wanted me to go as a woman. I purchased a pair of high-heeled shoes. Sam sprayed glue on them followed by plenty of silver glitter. He reached into his closet, found a dress for me, did my hair and make-up, and off we went.

I ran into another friend at the bar who was also dressed as a woman. We decided to leave the party early and go to the adult bookstore on the A1A strip and have some fun by hanging out on the corner with the prostitutes. As we took our positions on the street corner, we "struck a pose" for the cars idling at the traffic light. I noticed a hot guy in a pick-up truck laughing at us. The prostitutes weren't having it. They started yelling and cursing at us and ran us off. Maybe they were jealous of my shoes.

Later that year, Kurt and I planned a weekend stay in Orlando at a popular gay resort with a hotel, bars, entertainment, drag shows, and restaurants. I managed to secure a bag of pot and had about 25 joints in total. I packed my bag for the weekend, stashed the weed in the suitcase, and placed it under my bed. The plan was I would work my nightshift, go home, shower, and Kurt would pick me up and drive us to Orlando while I slept.

Arriving home that morning, I proceeded to pull the suitcase out from under the bed and the pot was missing. After frantically searching for it, I called my mother at the church and rudely said, "Where is it?!"

"Stay right there!" she said. "Your dad is on his way home!"

Not only was I grounded but I watched my mom flush the pot. A huge argument ensued and I told her I hated her. My weekend was ruined.

My father also found several gay romance novels I picked up from the adult bookstores hidden beneath my mattress and he wanted to know where I got them. While he wasn't angry, I could tell by his demeanor that he was concerned yet unsure how to address this issue but insisted I throw them away.

We had already gone through a "rid the house of rock music" phase weeks earlier when my father demanded my brothers and I bring all of our music to the dining room table so he could destroy everything. My brothers complied. When my father wasn't in the room, I browsed through my brothers' stash, grabbing everything I wanted. I took the whole collection to a friend's place, including the gay romance novels, until things blew over. My brothers lost their collection of music while I enlarged mine for free. I felt no guilt. As far as I was concerned, that was retribution for the gasoline-in-the-cup incident.

By now I had located several gay bars in different nearby towns. I had a system for which bars I would hit on the most popular nights, including adult bookstores for quick sex.

One afternoon, after a day at the beach, I decided to visit the adult bookstore on the A1A strip. Standing in the parking lot near my car, I met a guy whose band was touring. They were performing at one of the popular nightclubs and we hit it off. He was gay and asked me to go on tour with him. I declined because I knew my father would kill me if I pulled such a stupid stunt.

After he left, a Cuban man whistled and yelled out from above. I looked in his direction and he motioned for me to come up. I climbed the outside stairs of the seedy, dilapidated motel behind the adult bookstore, headed toward his room and, once inside, noticed how dark the room was. I saw another guy sitting in a chair by a table. He was either high on drugs, or drunk, or both. He looked like he had been run over by a train but I was attracted to him. I had an uneasy feeling about the guy who invited me in but nervously listened as he spoke.

They wanted to do a threesome. I was reluctant but agreed only because I was bored and had nothing better to do. Suddenly, there was a knock on the door. A white guy and a black female prostitute were standing there. She had made arrangements to use the room ahead of time and so the Cuban guy told me to get out. The threesome never happened.

Over two years had passed before my father was called to pastor a church in Kentucky. I decided to stay in Florida and moved in with the drag queen, Sam, and his partner. I also quit going to church.

My friend, Dave, called and suggested we go to Fort Lauderdale for the weekend. We took off and visited The Copa, a well-known gay bar in Fort Lauderdale. I met a guy and we hit it off. We exchanged phone numbers and stayed in touch, talking for several weeks. We decided to give it a shot as boyfriends and he suggested I move there. Dave wanted to move to Fort Lauderdale as well. So we talked about it and all three of us decided to share an apartment together.

# 6. Fort La~Di~Da

We moved in the summer of '84 to Fort Lauderdale, Florida, a spring break destination for thousands of college students. It was certainly a rowdy and festive time. Billy Idol's "Eyes Without a Face" dominated the local radio stations. Tina Turner was asking, "What's Love Got To Do With It," while Prince carried on about some doves crying. The guys and girls hit the beaches in festive-colored swim trunks and bikini's. They swarmed the beaches by day, the bars and clubs by night, many of them drunk and leaving trails of vomit along the sidewalks.

My boyfriend, Mac, found an apartment that wasn't exactly located in the safest area of Fort Lauderdale. A black drag queen and her white boyfriend lived across the courtyard from our apartment and they loved cocaine. He was hot. She was a tragic mess. They were friends with Mac who, unbeknownst to me, had a drug problem. I was repeatedly warned by others from the club scene that Mac went through guys like toilet paper. I wouldn't listen. *I was in love!*

Sure enough, one night I arrived home to find Mac in bed with another guy. He informed me that I would be sleeping on the couch. An argument ensued that turned physical. Dave called the police while Mac cornered me in the kitchen and held a butcher knife to my throat, threatening to slit it. The police arrived and no charges were filed, but Dave and I knew we had to move. A friend referred us to a guy who had a trailer for rent.

For months I practically lived at The Copa. I enjoyed seeing the occasional appearances of artists like Dale Bozzio, the lead singer of the group *Missing Persons*, who arrived at the club after a concert one night, or Gloria Gaynor who performed and assured us *she would survive*! It was thrilling to spot famous performers while watching the drag queens entertain the audience. The energy of the club, hundreds of hot guys, and great music made it a great place to hang out.

I worked three part-time jobs and trying to make ends meet was stressful. I lived off cigarettes, pizza, and baloney sandwiches. Fed up with being broke, I decided to visit a known hustler bar to see if I could pick up some extra money. "Hustling" is the male form of prostitution with a guy paying you for sex. I had no idea what to expect so I winged it. Some guys just wanted companionship while others wanted sex. I did whatever was asked of me but one encounter didn't go so well.

One night a man picked me up at this dive bar and drove me to his home in a deserted, wooded area on the outskirts of town. Once we were inside his place, he gave me a joint to smoke while he put on a porn tape. I had a high level of tolerance for drugs by now so I couldn't understand why, as I relaxed on the sofa smoking the joint, I started to feel ill. The man grabbed my hand and led me to the bedroom.

"Take off your clothes." he said, as we sat on his bed in the dimly lit bedroom.

"Where's the money?" I politely asked.

"What money?" he replied.

"The money I need because I'm struggling financially."

"You didn't mention I would be paying you for sex!"

I assumed he knew this would be a sex-for-cash transaction considering the reputation of the bar. I will never forget the way he glared at me. His eyes appeared almost black from rage.

"Take your clothes off and get naked on the bed while I get your money!" he demanded as he stood up, exited the room in a rush, slamming the bedroom door!

Something told me not to take my clothes off. I was scared and my mind was racing, unsure of what to do next. Not only was I feeling ill but the room was now spinning. I wondered if the joint had been laced with a more potent drug.

Panicked, I exited the bedroom and quickly walked toward the front door. The man was in the kitchen reaching inside one of the kitchen drawers. When he saw me he quickly slammed the drawer shut and pointed his finger toward the bedroom and yelled, "Get back in there!" Foolishly, I complied.

Back in the bedroom, sitting on the bed and staring at the wood paneling, I started to wonder if he was getting a knife. Perhaps the drug was making me paranoid. I was so confused and scared. Again, something told me to get out of there so I exited the bedroom again and made a quick dash through the living room to the front door. The guy cornered me. Shaking, I politely asked him to take me back to the bar. As he yelled and cursed, something told me to stay calm and say nothing. As he unleashed his fury, I apologized and said it was my fault. I hoped this would calm him down. It seemed to work. I politely asked him, again, to please take me back to the bar. Thankfully, he did.

On the drive back, he unleashed more of his fury and how I needed to be up front about my intentions. More expletives and insults were released as I sat quietly, trying to stay calm. I just stared out the window on that pitch-black night anxiously wanting to get away from this guy.

After exiting his car, I stood on the dark street next to the bar trying to absorb what just happened when another man drove up to the curb and rolled down his window. He wanted to take me back to his yacht and would pay for my time. Needing money, even after that scary experience, I got into the man's car.

The man drove to the marina. As we boarded his beautiful yacht, we started with small talk as he poured us a drink. That helped take my mind off of the prior incident. I finally started to relax. The guy told me what he wanted, I complied, and he paid me. I showered and he dropped me off at the bar. I drove home, exhausted, and climbed into bed.

One time a guy picked me up and drove me to his place. While there was no pressure for sex, he was willing to pay me to just lie in bed with him and cuddle and talk. I sensed he was lonely and in pain but I didn't want to "feel." That's why I medicated with drugs and alcohol. I didn't want to feel my own pain much less his! So I kept the conversation light until enough time had passed to warrant getting paid and then left. I had such conflicted emotions about what I was doing but I was trying to survive financially.

On another night, I met up with a friend and we parked across the street before heading into The Copa. We smoked weed in his car. As we were walking toward the club, I noticed a huge section of the road missing due to some construction work. I decided to jump across the deep hole. With one foot barely hitting the other side, I slipped and fell in the hole. My friend pulled me out and I was covered in dirt and blood. I hit the pavement hard. Being high, I didn't feel any pain. I noticed a white van parked across the street and asked if I was on *Candid Camera* and he laughed. I was taken into the women's restroom at the bar, cleaned up, and taken home.

God was about to get my attention. One night I was with a group of friends walking to the entrance of The Copa. As I listened to the other guys talking, the volume of everything around me was suddenly lowered and I clearly heard these words whispered in my ear, *"If you were to die tonight would you go to Hell?"* It stopped me in my tracks! Even though it was no more than a whisper, what I heard was very clear. I didn't mention it to the guys. They would have dropped me off at the nearest loony bin if I had proclaimed God had just spoken to me.

Some might question if it was God speaking but Christians know it is Satan's desire to destroy lives. If he had his way, *all of us* would spend eternity in Hell. Only God cares but I foolishly ignored His voice.

I had been living in Fort Lauderdale for approximately four months but it seemed like four years. I wasn't in touch with my family. My life revolved around clubs, drugs, drinking, and sex. What I used to consider off-limits or risky behavior was no longer a concern. I hardly had any boundaries left at this point because I was easily bored and always looking for new ways to break the monotony. I was open to trying anything for excitement and looking to fill the void inside, only to find everything was unfulfilling. I had been struggling with depression and couldn't mask the pain with drugs and alcohol any longer. One night, with no one around, I stood in the kitchen and held a bottle of Tylenol in my hand. I was seriously contemplating suicide but decided not to go through with it.

Being that I was rarely in contact with my family anymore, it was strange when my father called me out of the blue. During the course of the conversation he said it was time for me to come home. I didn't even argue. I was tired of life. My roommate, Dave, drove me back to Cocoa to say goodbye to my old friends before heading home to Kentucky.

Back in Cocoa, my drag queen friend, Sam, suggested we hit the bars and I was eager to because I could also say a bittersweet goodbye to the "old gang" I knew from the bar scene.

At one bar, I talked to an African-American guy who had always been friendly toward me. I mentioned I was moving to Kentucky to be with my family. Darrell mentioned he was going to

New York and asked if I would like to ride with him to keep him company. He said he would drop me off on the way. I agreed.

On the day of our departure, we packed up his white Cadillac and hit the road. Little did I know that there was a stretch of highway in Florida that was a known passageway used by drug traffickers to smuggle drugs. It wasn't long before a highway patrol officer started to follow us.

We were stopped and told to get out of the car before we were separated and questioned. I answered the officer's questions honestly. I don't know what Darrell told him but the officer had him unload the trunk of the car. The cop said our stories didn't match and proceeded to rummage through some of our luggage. I was nervous because I had no idea what he was looking for. After randomly searching various bags, he seemed satisfied and told us to repack the car and be on our way. On the road, Darrell said we were lucky because he had a weapon and cocaine in the trunk. He was moving the drugs to a contact in New York. By the grace of God, the cop missed them.

I met up with my family in Kentucky and it felt good to see them again. Darrell hit the road and I never heard from him again.

# 7. The Bluegrass State

Living with my family in Bowling Green, Kentucky, I slowly acclimated to life in middle-class suburbia with its slower pace and overly manicured lawns. I hung out with my siblings and met their friends, many of whom were into heavy metal music and smoked weed. Most of the time we just sat around and watched MTV.

I was bored to death living in this small town and it wasn't long before the depression and suicidal thoughts returned. The Internet didn't exist yet so finding gay bars was impossible. I didn't have friends, especially gay friends, a job, a car, or money. I felt alone and completely out of place. I would often walk around the mall, hoping to meet a gay guy without any luck.

One night I wandered into a bowling alley and started chatting with a guy and his girlfriend. He was friendly and I enjoyed talking to him since I was very lonely. When I told him I needed to leave, he offered to drive me home and told his girlfriend he would return shortly.

*"How very kind of him,"* I thought. *"Could he be bisexual? Why is he being so nice to me?"*

I didn't want him to take me directly to my house so I had him pull into a church parking lot close to my home.

"May I ask you a personal question?" I asked.

"Yes," he replied.

I probably sat there for at least a minute, stuttering, trying to get the nerve to ask if he was bisexual because I wanted to have sex with him.

*"What if he says no? What if he gets offended and assaults me?"* My mind raced with so many questions. Out of fear, I politely told him "Never mind, but thank you for the ride," and exited the car. We briefly exchanged glances as he drove away. The loneliness I felt was overwhelming and I started to cry as I walked the rest of the way home. Suicide seemed like the only answer to end the pain.

One evening, in the summer '84, I was sitting with my sister in the food court of the local mall. We were very close. I broke down and confessed to her that I was gay. I cried when I shared the news because I was afraid of her reaction. The news didn't seem to phase her. She said it didn't matter to her and that she loved me regardless. Her response gave me the courage to tell my brothers as well and they were equally supportive.

I awoke the next morning and decided it was time to tell my parents. Sitting at the dining room table, I shared the news. I was so afraid of what they would say. My mother told me she just wanted me to be happy.

My father didn't approve of homosexuality but didn't react in a negative way. He didn't seem to want to talk about it and I decided not to push the issue because I sensed he was uncomfortable with the news. Unlike the experience of many in the gay community who come out to their families, I'm thankful my family didn't disown me or kick me out of the house. I knew my family loved me.

My brother told me about an old family friend he was in touch with that wanted to see me. One Saturday morning I got up and drove to Clarksville, Tennessee, to visit her and her family.

Beth was a few years older than I was and my parents had known her family since we were little kids. Seeing her and catching up after many years was good for the soul. She worked for a government agency in downtown Nashville and encouraged me to apply for a job with the government.

# 8. The Last Train to Clarksville

Thanks to Beth's suggestion, I was hired for a data entry job with the government. Since my maternal grandparents lived in Clarksville, I moved in with them and started carpooling with friends and colleagues to Nashville to make the long commute tolerable. Finally, there seemed to be some stability in my life.

As a child, I'd spend weeks with my grandparents every summer. My grandmother and I got along very well and I really loved her. She always made me feel special. Sometimes she would let me play in her fancy dining room and pretend to have dinner with my make-believe friends while I wore her big clip-on earrings. She saw me doing this but never belittled or humiliated me for wearing her jewelry.

One day my grandfather surprised me with a used car he had purchased for $900. I secured a one-year loan from the bank in order to pay him back. He graciously co-signed for the loan since I didn't have established credit. I was thrilled to finally have a car and my new job.

I also learned there was a gay bar in Clarksville where I could meet guys and, hopefully, make some new friends. It was especially exciting when some of the military guys from Fort Campbell, Kentucky, would visit the bar. I'd venture out on weekends to spend time with one of the military dudes I had a crush on. The Pet Shop Boys released "West End Girls" and Dead or Alive's single, "You Spin Me Round (Like a Record)," moved gays onto the dance floor.

It was the mid-'80's but it was still dangerous to be gay in many parts of America, especially the South. A local drag queen had been murdered. You had to be aware of your surroundings due to ignorant rednecks who enjoyed beating up "faggots."

Having a drink at the bar one night, I heard a commotion. The gay guys near the front door said rednecks were blocking the entrance. I'm not sure if some type of altercation had occurred, but the gays were in a complete panic and I was one of them. Thankfully, the rednecks disappeared and the door opened again.

As thrilled as I was about my car and job, I couldn't shake the feelings of depression or suicidal thoughts. The car loan made me irritated because I knew I'd need to live one more year before I could pay if off. I wasn't always thinking clearly and made a lot of stupid mistakes, but I loved my grandfather and wasn't about to kill myself and stick him with my car loan. So, I "held on" for another year.

Late one night, I was at Beth's house. Her husband and children had gone to bed and she and I were deep in conversation in the kitchen. She started talking to me about the Lord. I don't know if she suspected I was gay. I had a hard time trusting people but broke down crying and told her my secret. I was sick of suffering in silence. She may not have understood homosexuality but she didn't judge me. Our conversation lasted until around 2:00 a.m. and she admitted she didn't actually know if homosexuality was a forgivable sin. I wasn't sure myself and believed I was resigned to burning in Hell because that's all I ever heard from "loving Christians."

After our talk, I started attending her church. I spoke with the pastor about rededicating my life to Christ and following it up (again) in baptism. I didn't know how to mesh my sexuality with my spirituality but I really wanted to please God.

I would eventually be re-baptized. I wanted to believe things would change and that I would no longer struggle with homosexuality. After the baptism, I sat in my car and looked up at the cloudy, overcast sky. While the rain gently hit the front windshield, I thanked God for giving me what I longed for...peace. Surely, this time things would be different. My hope was short-lived because I still struggled with a same-sex attraction. I wondered if my father was disappointed in me and if my Heavenly Father hated me because I was a homosexual.

I continued hitting the bars looking for love. I poured my energy into work while looking forward to meeting up with the military guy on the weekends. My depression lingered and thoughts of suicide grew stronger until I was mentally ready to go through with it.

I know many people consider suicide an incredibly selfish act. Personally, this is an unfair judgement because I never thought about killing myself as a way to hurt anyone. Trying to function normally on a daily basis, while struggling with severe depression, is unbearable. The sadness, hopelessness, and despair felt endless! Death seemed like the only way to *finally* be at peace.

Several months passed and when I received my monthly paycheck, I realized I could completely pay off my car loan. I decided I had better follow through with killing myself before my grandfather purchased something else.

# 9. Cancel the Hearse!

One morning when I was around the age of 14, my mother and I had a heated exchange and I lost it. I ran as fast as I could into the woods behind our home.

Deep inside the woods, I finally stopped running and started sobbing. I was overwhelmed and I wanted to scream! The desperation of wanting to escape my parents, school, bullies, being teased because of my looks, the desire to have friends, feeling alone while struggling with a same-sex attraction had reached a breaking point! Hiding out in the woods I could hear my mother calling my name but I didn't answer. I kept trying to figure out where to go to escape the pain I felt. As she continued to call my name, I left the woods and slowly walked toward the house where my father stood waiting for me. I was terrified of the whipping I knew was coming and looked at him like, "Go ahead! Hit me!" It didn't matter at that point because I already felt defeated. Surprisingly, my father didn't whip me. Instead, he told me to get ready for school.

Church was another issue. Inevitably, there would be a sermon on Sodom and Gomorrah. It pained me to hear about God's wrath on those two cities because of homosexuals.

One night my father was giving his own sermon and may have been preaching with no hidden agenda other than speaking about "sin," but I couldn't help but internalize it. I felt as if he was directing his words about Sodom and Gomorrah toward me. I was in such despair over my attraction to guys and remember seething with hatred toward my father, and God.  I didn't ask to be gay.  Who could I trust to discuss what I was struggling with?

I didn't have anyone to talk to about the bullying either.  I couldn't possibly tell my parents about it because I would have to disclose the words the kids were using against me.  I didn't know what their reaction would be.  I felt so much guilt and shame, suffering in silence.

*"Well I'm actually in a fairly good mood which is unusual 'cause, frankly, I'm often quite suicidal.  I went home the other night and stood upon my couch, tied the cord from my curtain around my neck, jumped off the couch and.......the curtains opened."*
**— Comedian Paula Poundstone**

On July 2, 1985, without my grandparents noticing, I took a new bottle of aspirin from the kitchen cabinet, grabbed my cigarettes, a cold glass of sweet tea and walked outside.  I closed the door behind me and stood beside the entrance to the garage.  The silence on that warm, summer night was almost deafening.  There was just enough light coming from the moon to see shadows from the neighborhood houses.

I lit a cigarette and stared up at the sky.  I wondered what Heaven was like.  I wondered what it was like to be at peace.  I also started to cry because I feared death.  After finishing the cigarette,

I swallowed nearly half of the bottle of aspirin, and then I panicked. I had changed my mind but now it was too late. How could I go inside and confess to my grandparents what I had just done? Instead, I walked back into the house to refill my glass with tea before returning outside to quickly swallow the remainder of the aspirin, all 100 of them. I stared at the moon as I smoked one last cigarette. I walked into the house, crawled into my bed to go to sleep and, hopefully, die.

I couldn't fall asleep. I faded in and out of consciousness. My mind was fuzzy, images of fire and the rock group, KISS, flashed before my eyes. I wasn't even a fan of their music. Why didn't I have visions of Motley Crüe, whom I loved? I also had a weird sensation as though the middle of my body was sinking into the bed. As I became more aware of the reality of the situation, I started tossing and turning.

At some point there was a loud ringing in my ears that was driving me nuts. It was around 3:00 a.m. when I made myself get up to go outside and smoke another cigarette. I kept thinking at any second I would go to sleep and never wake up again. Eventually, I crawled back into bed and finally passed out or fell asleep. I had no idea how much time passed but the next thing I knew my grandmother was trying to wake me up to go to work.

Feeling like I had been run over by a train, I dragged myself to the bathroom and started throwing up. My grandmother thought it was food poisoning and rushed me to the emergency room. Since I made it through the night, the doctor didn't pump my stomach. He said the aspirin would need to work its way out of my system. I was in agony and my head ached. The slightest noise was magnified and the ringing in my ears was unbearable. I believe the doctor said it had to do with the aspirin I ingested, but it would subside in time.

The doctor refused to release me from the hospital unless I told my grandmother what I had done, or else visit a nearby psychiatric clinic for evaluation. I chose the clinic. I didn't want to hurt my grandmother by telling her the truth.

My grandmother drove me to the clinic. I was evaluated by two counselors. One threatened to put me in a psychiatric ward at the hospital immediately. She repeated what the doctor at the hospital said. I could only go home if I told my grandmother what I had done. She needed to know my grandmother would keep an eye on me. I agreed. It pained me to tell my grandmother, especially when she started crying. The counselor also warned that my suicidal thoughts would likely increase and I would start imagining new ways to kill myself to ensure the next time I would succeed.

What I had just experienced was agonizing so I dismissed what the counselor said and told myself suicide wasn't the answer. She was right. Within two weeks the suicidal thoughts came back and were even stronger than before. I considered finding a gun. That frightened me because I had already decided I would never use a gun. With my luck, I would only blow half my head off and live, and then have bad hair days for the rest of my life. Gays can be judgmental when it comes to bad hairstyles.

When I finally returned to work, a co-worker asked if I wanted to grab some lunch. He was gay, African-American, Christian, and we became fast friends. Paul later said God told him we would be close. Since he'd already overheard many of the angry conversations I'd had with a Christian lady at work, he didn't have a very high opinion of me. That poor woman at work did her best to show me love while keeping me on track with God. She was patient and listened as I spewed venom concerning my thoughts about "Christians." I hated them and was mad at God. I resented the despair I felt regarding my same-sex attraction. Thankfully, she was patient and never gave up on me and we have a close friendship to this day.

Paul and I developed a great friendship over the course of a year. He wanted to move to Los Angeles, where his godmother lived, to pursue his love of music and acting. We discussed going together and I told my family. We packed our cars and were on our way to Los Angeles. Telling my family goodbye and seeing their tears was hard. I knew I would miss them.

# 10. Welcome to the Jungle

Paul and I eventually arrived in South Central Los Angeles. I met his godmother, who was from the South. She was a very sweet woman, in her late 40's, who was easy-going and still had all her Southern charm. Her warm smile immediately put me at ease. She agreed to let us stay at her place until we found jobs. Her tiny studio apartment was warm and inviting, with a Buddhist shrine to the right as you entered the door.

She warned that we should remove everything from our cars that night because if we didn't, odds were that it wouldn't be there in the morning. The streets nearby were lined with middle-class homes but the area where we lived was a little sketchy. I didn't understand why helicopters often hovered very low and shined their lights into our windows. I thought, "What a great neighborhood watch program they have!" I later learned it was because the police were looking for gang members or someone who had just committed a crime.

Approximately six years later, Reginald Denny, a white truck driver, would nearly be beaten to death not far from where we lived during the infamous L.A. riots.

By then, Paul and I had found jobs and moved into a one-bedroom apartment in North Hollywood, in the San Fernando Valley, just north of Los Angeles.

I was working for A&M Records, an independent record label owned and run by Herb Alpert from the well-known group,

Herb Alpert & the Tijuana Brass, and Jerry Moss. Herb's hits included the song, "This Guy's In Love With You," and "Diamonds," featuring vocals by Janet Jackson. A&M's roster of artists included The Carpenters, Simple Minds, Soundgarden, Sting, The Police, Nazareth, Janet Jackson, Sheryl Crow, Bryan Adams, Iggy Pop, the Brothers Johnson, Peter Frampton and others. The offices were at La Brea Avenue and Sunset Boulevard on the grounds of what was once the original Charlie Chaplin studio.

A&M Records consisted of several small buildings on a large lot but not all of them were connected. Sometimes it was necessary to go outside to reach another building. This provided an opportunity to see artists from other record labels who were recording in the numerous A&M studios. During my time at A&M, I ran into Rod Stewart, Sting, Chrissie Hynde from The Pretenders, David Crosby, Bruce Springsteen, and some of the guys from Aerosmith. On one occasion I followed Janet Jackson into the art department while stumbling upon comedian Sam Kinison, who was lost and looking for the studio. Upstairs in the promotions department, I once opened an office door to find Barry White sitting there comfortably, enjoying a cigarette. Beside him was a platter of fruit and champagne. He smiled and, through the cloud of smoke, asked me to join him.

One of the most memorable moments was when the group, Sounds of Blackness, performed during a lunchtime concert and I spotted Nikki Sixx and Tommy Lee from the heavy metal band, Motley Crüe, sitting on the steps in front of the studio. Someone had already tipped me off that Motley Crüe was in the studio recording their next album so I kept one of their early albums with me at all times in case I ran into them. I quickly grabbed it, walked over to them, and they kindly signed the album. As I walked away, I was so happy I started crying. I had been a fan of the band for years but never thought I would actually meet them. My only disappointment was I didn't meet the lead singer, Vince Neil, as I had a huge crush on him.

My gay friends never understood why I was into Motley Crüe and other heavy metal bands but shunned show tunes. To me, Barbra Streisand was some singer who did a duet with Donna Summer, and I didn't even know who Judy Garland was. I think they secretly wanted to claw my eyes out.

The record business started going through a transitional period and independent labels were being purchased by major labels. It wasn't long before A&M was sold to Polygram Records and I landed a job on the publishing side. Our receptionist at the time, Cheri Oteri, would later go on to be a regular on *Saturday Night Live*. She would often entertain us by imitating how we spoke or walked when delivering our messages.

Donny and Marie Osmond had a talk show so I managed to get a ticket. Fans in the audience (including me) had their Donny and Marie memorabilia in hand. Donny and Marie eventually appeared and I turned into a giddy schoolgirl when I saw Donny. When the show was over, a security guard motioned for everyone to exit the studio. I wasn't leaving without meeting Donny. When the security guard turned his head, I made a quick dash onto the floor and shoved an item into Donny's hand. He graciously autographed his album and I left the studio in disbelief that I'd finally met my childhood idol.

During this time, I longed to be in church. I felt so empty, like something was missing. I had a deep desire for God but felt God had no desire for me because I was a homosexual.

Paul and I considered ourselves a couple but intimacy was difficult because I struggled with whether or not homosexuality was a sin. He didn't. After seven years together, we split up and I moved out and found a place of my own. He deserved someone who was at peace with his sexual orientation. I needed space to try and figure things out.

I found a church I liked and would leave after the service. I didn't trust Christians. I only wanted to hear the Word of God. I eventually let my guard down and attended a Young Adult Singles class. As time passed, I slowly became more involved and was asked to help in certain areas. It made me happy to feel like part of the team. I joined the choir and regularly attended Sunday morning, evening, and Wednesday night services.

I figured if I threw myself into church work, I could "earn" God's love and approval. Perhaps He wouldn't be angry with me because I was a homosexual. The verse, "For by grace you have been saved through faith. And this is not your own doing; it is the gift of God, *not a result of works* (emphasis added), so that no one may boast." (Ephesians 2:8-9), had yet to sink into my thick head.

The constant struggle between my faith and my same-sex attraction was mentally and emotionally exhausting. Choose Christ or choose love because you can't have both if it's with a man! My depression continued and the suicidal thoughts returned. There were months when it was a struggle to simply get out of bed to go to work. Many days I would just lie in bed and cry.

In desperation, I reached out to the pastor at my church. I didn't sense any judgment from him as he listened. He prayed with me and gave me some information on a well-known ex-gay ministry. I was a little suspicious when I heard the "success stories" from members of this group. I guessed by dating and/or marrying the opposite sex they successfully gave the appearance of being reformed but, at the core, they were probably still homosexuals.

If God truly detested homosexuality under all circumstances, and gays like myself were crying, begging, pleading for deliverance, then why was He changing *some* homosexuals to heterosexuals but not others? It didn't make any sense. I thought perhaps God was selective and maybe deliverance was conditional after all. Maybe I wasn't good enough, perfect enough, holy enough, righteous enough, or didn't have His favor. I became resentful toward God because I wanted answers.

Nearly two decades later, a former chairman of that same now defunct organization admitted his sexual orientation never truly changed and apologized for the pain he caused. It was unfortunate so many of us struggled unnecessarily when other

Christians used the organization as proof we absolutely "chose" to be homosexual.

On Sunday and Wednesday nights I would leave church and often frequent an adult bookstore nearby and hook up with men in cars on dark, secluded streets. It was risky behavior but I craved affection. I was conflicted and couldn't deal with the struggle anymore. It wasn't long before I left the church.

Months later, I stumbled upon information about a small Bible study in West Hollywood attended by gay men who professed to be Christian as well.

A popular drag queen told me about a *gay* church he attended in North Hollywood and I decided to check it out. It was important for me to find a church that showed reverence to God because it's about Him, not us. I also didn't want God's Word changed to fit *my* needs. My desire was to really know what God's Word had to say about homosexuality. The church appeared to have everything I was looking for even if the pastor's interpretation of the Word of God concerning homosexuality differed from what I was raised to believe.

During this time, many Christians were starting to address the issue of homosexuality and same-sex marriage. In the theological debates I heard, heterosexual Christians couldn't come to an agreement. Some believed it was wrong while others thought same-sex marriage was okay if it was in a committed, monogamous relationship, and were certain that scripture in the Bible concerning homosexuality had been taken out of context.

The same was true for homosexuals debating the issue. Many thought "the act" itself was wrong and were leading a life of celibacy while others felt it was okay to be in a committed, monogamous, same-sex relationship. The most exasperating part for me was that everyone seemed to speak with such authority and backed up their particular stance with God's Word. On numerous occasions I would pour my heart out to God, with deep, guttural, sobbing pleas for Him to give me peace about the issue. I didn't know what to believe.

My father drove to Los Angeles for a visit. I took him to my new church hoping he might change his thoughts on homosex-uality when he saw gay people worshiping God. It was a mistake that resulted in a huge blowout by the time we reached Beverly Hills for lunch. He said it was wrong and wouldn't let up. I was so tired of struggling with feeling conflicted that I yelled at him and started sobbing. Lunch was quiet as neither of us had much to say.

Not long after, I wrote my father a letter trying to find a way for us to make peace with the issue but the conversation proved futile and I eventually cut off communication.

# 11. This Is No Dream. It's Really Happening!

When I was around the age of five, my father was pastor of a church in Indian Mound, Tennessee. After a Wednesday night church service, the choir began rehearsal for Sunday's morning service. I was lying on a church pew, relaxing, and listened as the choir sang. My eyes were suddenly drawn to a small circle of red lights moving in a circular direction around what looked like a silver fire sprinkler embedded in the ceiling of the church.

I suddenly "disconnected" from my body, experiencing a floating sensation as I drifted toward the red lights, through the ceiling, and quickly found myself surrounded by white light. I knew I was not alone as "others" were around me having a discussion. The conversation was not audible. The messages were being sent telepathically and I could hear their conversation in my head. I wasn't privy to the discussion, as I didn't understand the language being spoken. I had no idea how much time passed but when "they" finished their conversation, I floated back and reconnected to my body.

The most unique thing about the experience was the overwhelming love I felt. It was like nothing I had ever experienced on earth. I actually stayed on the church pew and *begged* It (whatever "It" was) to take me back! That *love* was powerful and I wanted to feel it again!

Approximately 25 years after that out-of-body experience, I was preparing lunch in my apartment when the memory hit me like a bolt of lightning. It occurred to me that when I got up from the church pew as a child, I never thought about that incredible experience again. It was as though the memory was removed and was now being returned to me for some reason. All I could conclude from that moment was *maybe* it was a confirmation from God that He has been with me all along. Perhaps He hasn't given up on me. I was hopeful.

# 12. Hinduism

I longed for a relationship with God but I also wanted peace with Him concerning my same-sex attraction. I wasn't going to get that by being a traditional Southern Baptist. Perhaps I could settle the issue through another religion.

There was a New Age bookstore in town I'd often visit. I would spend hours browsing through various books on alternative religions, psychic phenomenon, even occult and New Age teachings, while meditation music softly filled the air, open to anything that spoke to me.

The bookstore had a variety of amulets, crystals, incense, talismans, anointing oils, potions, candles, and other items required for rituals or casting spells. Psychics were available for those seeking answers and I often met with one and had my tarot cards read despite the verse, "Let no one be found among you...who practices divination or sorcery, interprets omens, engages in witchcraft, or cast spells, or who is a medium or spiritist" (Deuteronomy 18:10-11). This is "...evil in the eyes of the Lord, provoking Him to anger" (2 Chronicles 33:6).

At the time, I didn't see what I was doing as something that was not in God's will or that I could possibly be "provoking Him to anger." People mentioned in the Bible who practiced this "evil" were enemies of God. I didn't consider myself an enemy of God. God knew my heart. I was sincerely trying to find Him because I had questions.  I never thought about how I secured those answers as being a problem.

While browsing in the bookstore one evening, I came across a book entitled, *Journey to Self-Realization*, by an Indian yogi and guru, Paramahansa Yogananda, who introduced millions of Westerners to the teachings of meditation and Kriya yoga. *

It seemed like he knew God intimately, and I longed to know God the same way he described his relationship with God.  But was his "god" the God I believed in?  I was encouraged by the words of Yogananda and delved into Hinduism.  I was optimistic because I thought maybe Yogananda's teachings would help point the way to a more direct path that would guarantee a *supernatural* experience with God, with the added bonus of not having to associate with judgmental Christians.

---

* A meditation technique that quickly accelerates one's spiritual growth, and whose devoted practice is supposed to lead to the realization of God, union with the Divine, and liberation of the soul from all forms of bondage.  For anyone considering practicing any form of yoga, even for health reasons, I suggest you do your research on "the dangers of yoga," especially Kundalini yoga, including the spiritual deception of "Christian yoga."  Yoga is rooted in Hindu occultism.  I recommend the book, *Death of a Guru* by Rabindranath R. Maharaj, a descendant from a long line of Brahmin priests and trained as a yogi.  He details the deception, contact with demons, and what led to his conversion from Hinduism to Christianity, as well as *Out of India*, by Caryl Matrisciana, who details her journey through Hinduism and the New Age movement.  You can find numerous videos of her testimony on YouTube as well.

I decided to attend a Sunday morning service at the Self-Realization Temple in Hollywood, which was founded by Yogananda.

I took a seat and noticed a row of photos of guru's displayed at the front: Bhagavan Krishna, Mahavatar Babaji, Lahiri Mahasaya, Paramahansa Yogananda, and Swami Sri Yukteswar. The line-up also included a (man-made image) photo of Jesus in the middle. I was uneasy with the fact they were all apparently on the same level as Jesus.

Through my studies and from what I understood, Hinduism does not advocate the worship of any one particular deity. It teaches we are not accountable to a "Christian God" that requires judgment on sin. Any wrongdoing is considered to be done out of ignorance. The gods and goddesses of Hinduism are many.

Hindus believe in the Vedas (similar to theology books), including the Bhagavad Gita (the Hindu's Holy Testament or "bible"). Christianity, however, believes in the final authority of God's Word. Hindus are generally respectful of the Bible. In the services I attended, I was surprised, and delighted, that scripture from God's Word was read in addition to other sacred Hindu texts.

Many Hindus respect Jesus as the founder of modern Christianity. Because God's Word is silent about Jesus' teenage years until His public ministry at age 30, many Hindus believe that Jesus spent his educational years in India, learning a variety of yogic paths in order to teach and help mankind.

Hindus don't see Jesus as the *only way* to God even though Jesus made that claim (John 14:6).  Hindus also do not believe that mankind has been reconciled to God because of what Jesus did on the Cross:  "Neither is there salvation in any other: for there is none other name under Heaven given among men, whereby we must be saved" (Acts 4:12).

One of the spiritual goals of a Hindu is to achieve "Moksha" (which is emancipation/liberation/release from rebirth).  Until Moksha is achieved, a Hindu believes that he or she will be repeatedly reincarnated to pay back the negative actions (karma) of one's life.  It is achieved by your own efforts; a Hindu has to work for Moksha.

There are similar beliefs between Hinduism and Christianity.  Hindus believe in karma (the law of cause and effect by which each individual creates his own destiny by his thoughts, words and deeds) versus God's Word, which warns that our actions have consequences:  "Whatsoever a man sows, that he will also reap" (Galatians 6:7).  However, they are not the same.  For a Christian, our experiences in life are not consequences of one's own *past* actions.  God's Word doesn't support reincarnation.  We live only once:  "And as it is appointed unto men once to die, but after this the judgment" (Hebrews 9:27).

I found reincarnation to be both physical *and* mental enslavement, driving one to despair, working tirelessly to reach perfection, which can never be attained.  Having studied God's Word over the years, I knew enough to know that we, as human beings, would never reach God's standard of perfection. Satan wants us to be deceived by believing we can work to earn our salvation.

Even if I wasn't a Christian, or "religious," from a practical standpoint I found the concept of reincarnation to be a cruel joke. It doesn't even give you the knowledge of past mistakes in order to do better in your next life. There was no consolation that you would ever reach Moksha. How can reincarnation bring comfort when I can be assured of eternal life *by a Savior who did all the work for me on the Cross?*

When I took everything into consideration, I couldn't overlook the fact that Hinduism failed to recognize Jesus as the only source of salvation for humanity. To me, no one would ever be equal to, or above, Jesus. While I may have been searching for answers, and open to how I would find them, I was determined to avoid Christians.

# 13. The God Dilemma

I accept that it's difficult for some people to believe that there *is* a living God. However, there are some fundamental truths that I learned about God that I would like to share in order for the satanic lies and deception to be exposed.

God longs to have a genuine relationship with us (Revelation 3:20; John 14:23). We, as human beings, want someone to love us unconditionally, not out of guilt or force. It is the same way with God. He doesn't want robots. God made it clear there is only *one way* He can have a relationship with us and further explanation as to *why* and *how* will be explained later.

While on Earth we are given a gift called *life*. Somewhere along the way we will be confronted with the knowledge of something beyond this existence. In order to have a creation there must be a Creator (Genesis 1:1; Psalm 19:1; Romans 1:20-21). The biggest obstacle for many is the belief in the one and only true living God. While there are many gods, and many paths to those gods, they are either man-made idols, or deceased men who once proclaimed themselves to be "god."

Many believe we evolved, for instance, from an ape or other life forms. I love and appreciate animals and feel they are a gift from God because they bring unconditional love and companionship to so many. However, when one looks at the differences between man and animals, perhaps one will see that there is something beyond human comprehension at work in this great universe and that there *is* a personal, knowable God who "created mankind in His own image" (Genesis 1:27; 2:7), while animals are not.

The difference between human beings and animals is that animals do not have souls. Jesus didn't die for the sins of animals. Animals have limited understanding. They do not know if they are a cow or an elephant, male or female. An animal doesn't have the ability to decide if it has enough time to cross a street before being hit by a car, or that killing is murder. Humans understand the concept of right and wrong, that choices have consequences, and can show remorse. Animals do not. An animal does not possess a yearning for God. Mankind does. To evolve from an ape, we would not have these abilities. This is what separates us from animals.

Many believe the Bible is nothing more than made-up stories written by men. The Bible is a revelation of God to man, revealing His quest for man, not man's desire for God (2 Timothy 3:16; Romans 1:20). The Bible, which consists of 66 books, was written by 40 authors over a 1500+ year time span. It was written by men from different time periods, from various occupations, who resided on three different continents: Africa, Asia and Europe. It could not have delivered God's perfect message *with consistency* without some sort of *supernatural* inspiration (2 Timothy 3:16; 2 Peter 1:19-21). How can man write about God? It has to be by divine inspiration.

If, for example, I randomly chose 66 books, from 40 different authors, on three different continents, over a 1,500 year time span, on what causes depression and how to treat it, I know I would not find consistency in their findings and suggestions for treatment. That's what makes the Bible so unique.

If one looks at the complexity of the human body, the planet Earth, the animal kingdom, or even the vastness of the universe, there must be a Creator. Because of gravity, everything must come down. What keeps the planets from falling and/or crashing into each other? Scientists can answer this question any way they see fit but their explanation must give credit to a Creator who designed it that way.

# 14. Woe Unto You Hypocrites
### (Matthew 23:13-33)

While I continued to explore other teachings, something in my spirit wouldn't allow me any peace. It was like God kept pointing me back to a Bible-believing, Christ-centered church but I didn't want to be around Christians. The church should be a place where individuals can safely bare their souls and discuss their struggles. However, I knew from experience this was not possible.

It was disappointing to see Sunday School classes for those going through a divorce but not for those struggling with a same-sex attraction. Churches go out of their way to help with the recovery process for divorced individuals, including spiritual guidance and emotional healing. Additionally, they have the added bonus of finding others who've been through this so they can find a strong support system. I couldn't understand why homosexuals were deprived of a similar class at church. It would have helped me tremendously to meet others who were also struggling with a same-sex attraction.

What many Christians fail to understand is that homosexuals, who have given their lives to Christ, walk a very lonely road. Most Christians detest us because we're gay, and gays avoid us because we're Christian. A support group for homosexuals in a *safe* Christian environment would help many stay the course with God while working through various issues. So many kids struggle with their sexuality. Because of confusion, fear, and having no one to talk to, the despair and hopelessness can be overwhelming. To some, suicide seems like the only answer.

Heterosexuals will never understand what we go through as LGBT individuals. It has been ingrained in our minds that we are perverts, an abomination, that God hates us, that He created AIDS to kill the fags, and that we're going to Hell. Many have been betrayed, bullied, disowned by family and/or friends, even kicked out of homes and churches. In many parts of the United States, people have been murdered simply because they were a homosexual. Laws in certain parts of the world have been enacted to kill us.

We learn early on to wear many faces, to be "actors," play the game, trust no one. We sacrifice sanity and self-worth daily in order to fit in, to be loved and accepted. We struggle to find our place in society. This is part of the reason why so many of us develop depression, medicate with drugs or alcohol, and commit suicide. Who, in their right mind, would choose this life?

I have had women, who knew I was gay, offer me sex with no strings attached because they wanted to see if they could "convert" me into a heterosexual. I turned them down. That's the kind of offer most heterosexual men dream about. Heterosexuals need to understand this isn't about sex. We do not have "on" and "off" buttons for who we are attracted to.

Numerous Christian pastors have sounded the alarm of impending judgment on America because of homosexuality, yet little is said about the alarming divorce rate, adultery, porn, idolatry, even the millions of aborted babies in America.

I understand many Christians are resistant to the idea of welcoming homosexuals into their churches for fear that homosexuals will demand approval of their lifestyle, causing dissension, influencing children, sexually hitting on a church member, etc. That's a valid concern. For me, I merely wanted a safe place to hear the Word of God without being mistreated.

Yes, Christians have an obligation to tell people about sin. The difference between Jesus and many Christians today is He didn't mistreat people. A true act of love is treating someone with respect and kindness while explaining that sin is to be hated, not excused or taken lightly (Ephesians 4:15; 1 Peter 3:15).

To parents and church leaders, if you really care about the lives of every young boy and girl, throwing them out of homes and churches will only push them into a world where there are wolves waiting to devour them. Love these children and try to keep them on course with God. It's not the job of the heterosexual Christian to change the homosexual. *If any change is going to happen concerning the natural orientation of a homosexual, that can only come as a result of the power of the Holy Spirit.* Did you choose to be heterosexual? Of course you didn't.

Nowhere in God's Word does it tell us we have to be perfect to attend church. The church has a fundamental duty to welcome and *love* each individual and treat them with respect. That doesn't mean you are being asked to "love their sin."

# 15. Woe Unto You Hypocrites
## (Part Deux)

In fairness to the Christian community, the hypocrisy of the LGBT community also needs to be addressed.  The issue of Christian businesses being targeted with lawsuits by some LGBT individuals, because the Christian owner refused to offer a service simply because he or she didn't want to go against his or her religious beliefs, is on the rise.  And this was before the Supreme Court ruling on same-sex marriage in June 2015.

Google these phrases for numerous, disturbing reports:

"Christians arrested for saying homosexuality is a sin"

"Christian businesses sued by homosexuals"

"Homosexual persecution of Christians"

The real hypocrisy was exposed when a Christian contacted thirteen pro-gay bakeries asking each one to include "Gay Marriage Is Wrong" on a cake.  Not one bakery complied with his request.  He was met with insults and obscenities.  After his experiment, he was bombarded with hate messages about how "hateful" he was for simply giving them a taste of their own medicine.  The gentleman said, *Here is our point.  A Christian making a homosexual cake with 'Support Gay Marriage' goes against his faith, and a homosexual putting 'Gay Marriage Is Wrong' goes against his faith as well.  Now, of course we honor their right to say no; this is not the issue, but what about honoring the Christian's right to also say no?*

Can you imagine the outrage if this man had chosen to sue all thirteen of those bakeries? Yes, we need to find a common sense solution that not only protects the LGBT community from discrimination but also protects religious freedom.

Members of the LGBT community need to understand that not all Christians are anti-gay. Many Christians have gay family members, gay friends, gay co-workers, with many being fans of gay celebrities like Ellen DeGeneres and Elton John. A Christian following his or her conscience and religious beliefs is not a hateful, direct attack on homosexuals. A church unwilling to support same-sex marriage is not discrimination. There are Christians who are simply following their hearts and doing what they feel is in alignment with God's will.

Also disturbing were photos distributed on the Internet of a gay pride parade where homosexual men were dressed like Jesus, hanging on a cross, and kissing someone of the same sex. I don't believe it was meant as a generalized statement against religion because I didn't see any similar photos of Buddha, Mohammed, or Hindu gods. To those who make a mockery of Jesus, disregarding what He means to millions of people around the world, it is inappropriate, distasteful, and disrespectful...not only to homosexuals who have a strong faith in Christ but to heterosexual Christian *allies* of the LGBT community.

Why was there outrage by LGBT activists over someone refusing to issue a same-sex marriage license when little outrage was displayed over the two gay men who were alleged to have been murdered by a radical Muslim in Seattle?  What about the video footage of ISIS members throwing gay men to their deaths from the roof of a building in the Middle East, or gay men being publicly hanged from a crane in Iran?  Christians are attacked, sued, jailed, and fired for merely stating their belief that "homosexuality is a sin" while gay rights advocates turn a blind eye to Islam's teaching that homosexuality is punishable by *death*.

The Democratic Party quietly supports Islam and a Muslim invasion that has practically destroyed Sweden, Germany, France and the U.K.  Women and LGBT individuals are sounding the alarm as to what is happening in their countries.  Imams have made it clear that Muslims should implement Sharia *worldwide*.  Sharia teaches that homosexuality *is a vile form of fornication, punishable by death*.  This is why countless LGBT individuals are defecting from the Democratic party, hence the successful #WalkAway Campaign.  Google/YouTube for more information.

The LGBT community's anger toward the Christian community is understandable but two wrongs don't make a right.  This is an opportunity to show Christians what it means to "love thy neighbor" (Mark 12:31).  A good place to start is by supporting gay-friendly businesses that would welcome the opportunity to provide the services you are looking for while respecting the religious beliefs of others.

# 16. Back to the Lion's Den

It became clear that I needed to find a church home. I was hurting and wanted answers. I visited several churches and was frustrated by what I saw happening in the churches.

Many churches had turned into contemporary worship services with rock bands. There was a time when worship services used hymns that spoke of the blood of Jesus and the Cross. Now it was more about the performance than about Jesus. Pastors were trying to appear "hip" ("Be not conformed to this world..." Romans 12:2) while worship teams tried to emulate rock concerts.

I heard messages from pastors, even televangelists, preaching the "prosperity gospel" in which all you had to do was "name it and claim it." The way they preached made it sound like God was on standby, ready to jump through hoops like a little genie to ensure you had a mansion, a fleet of cars, and a fat bank account. Health would be restored and all your problems would disappear if you only had faith. I'm not a theologian but I knew this was nonsense. Nothing is impossible with God, but He will not be used in this manner. The unfortunate part is when God doesn't deliver on the demands of self-serving people, they become disillusioned and dare to question God. The problem is not God. The problem is the motive of the individual thinking he or she can use or manipulate God.

I wasn't going to church to be coddled or to use God for my selfish desires. I wasn't concerned about my self-esteem; I could see a therapist for that. I wanted guidance on escaping the insanity that was my life. I didn't know how to get back on track with God and was frustrated that I wasn't hearing how to do that.

In hindsight, I knew a few decades ago, there were fearless pastors who spoke about sin and the consequences of our choices. Instructions were provided on how to live a life that is pleasing to God. They explained the purpose of Jesus' life, the real meaning behind the shed blood of Christ on the Cross, the urgency in making a decision for Christ concerning our salvation, sharing the Gospel with others, and the reality of Hell for unrepentant sinners who rejected Christ.....and the churches were packed! Now the pulpits are filled with spineless pastors who have succumbed to political correctness, water down God's Word, and refuse to speak the truth to the masses for fear of offending people even though souls are at stake.

It was clear. Most pastors didn't fear God anymore and most Christians didn't want to hear truth. They only wanted to hear what made them feel good. It was prophesied, before the return of Jesus, what conditions would be like in this world: "For the time will come when they will not endure sound doctrine; but after their own lusts shall they heap to themselves teachers, having itching ears. And they shall turn away their ears from the truth, and shall be turned unto fables" (2 Timothy 4:3-4; Jude 1:17-19).

Many of us are hungry for God's Word and *want* to feel uncomfortable and convicted by the Holy Spirit if it will help in our spiritual growth and our walk with God. That's how we grow as Christians. *If people do not hear about sin and its consequences, there can be no conviction and repentance.*

Pastors, you are called to preach the uncompromising Word of God. That means all of it, including the uncomfortable parts. It's unfortunate you get more "meat" from cults, false religions, and New Age teachings than you do at the House of God.

Frustrated, fed-up, and disillusioned, I left the church again. I sank into another bout of depression and the suicidal thoughts returned.

# 17. Hello Darkness, My Old Friend

One night the suicidal thoughts were so strong that I drove to a local Christian bookstore to find books on the topic of suicide from a Biblical perspective. I didn't know if it was a forgivable sin in God's eyes. The fear of Hell was the one thing that kept me from following through with it again even though, with the first suicide attempt, that thought wasn't at the forefront of my mind. I have no idea why.

I couldn't find any books on the subject and sat on the floor in a back section of the store where no one could see me, and cried. It wasn't for attention. I just wanted the pain, the despair, and the hopelessness to go away. I sincerely wanted to die. I wanted peace! Thankfully, the store was practically empty because it was nearly closing time.

At that point in my life, I lived in a place by the beach, worked in Beverly Hills, had traveled to various destinations around the world, drove a fancy car, and met countless politicians, celebrities, and rock stars. I had spent years in the clubs enjoying drugs and sexual encounters with hundreds of guys. To some, it might have appeared like I "had it all" but, honestly, on the inside I was in despair, broken, and suicidal. The world had nothing to offer me that I found fulfilling.

After about four years of not communicating with my father, he called one night when I was contemplating suicide again. Why he called I have no idea, but I didn't care. I broke down and cried because I needed him. He patiently listened as I explained what was going on and I agreed to visit him soon.

Months later, I flew home to see my father and our time together was enjoyable. Conversations still arose about my same-sex attraction but they were civil. My father asked questions and made an effort to try and understand the best he could. Our relationship was growing and was better than it had ever been.

I finally understood my father's lack of approval regarding homosexuality wasn't a personal attack on me. He was concerned about my relationship with God, my salvation, and where I would spend eternity. I got it. He loved me!

I also don't blame my parents for being gay. My siblings are all heterosexual and I happen to be homosexual. It was futile to try and understand why I was a homosexual.

# 18. I'm Gonna Wash That ~~Gray~~ Gay Right Out of My Hair!

All my life I've struggled to understand God's Word. Thankfully, I found a church in the San Fernando Valley that had a group Bible study every Monday night. The way the teachers presented the information was exactly what my simple mind needed. They helped me understand the context in which the Bible was written. I diligently stayed with the Bible study for almost two years.

A friend invited me to visit a church in the San Gabriel Valley. The pastor of this church was concerned with how members of the LGBT community were being treated by the Christian community. He eventually approved having a support group at the church designed specifically for members of the LGBT community. I never thought I would see this in a Baptist church. Thankfully, when the class met, fire and brimstone didn't fall from the sky.

It was encouraging to hear others share their journeys, often told with tears. Their stories brought back memories of when I would visit with gay friends who cried as they shared painful stories of how Christians, even family members, treated them because they were homosexual. One of my struggling gay friends, who believed in Jesus, shared the health issues he suffered trying to reconcile the two only to suffer from depression and epileptic seizures. He attempted suicide and landed involuntary in a mental health hospital. He was told by a Christian friend and colleague to castrate himself. He was even told by another individual that he should commit suicide. Where is the compassion even if it's just to pray with those struggling with homosexuality?

One night after work, I stopped at a local restaurant to grab some dinner and struck up a conversation with a guy who happened to be a Christian. He invited me to join a Bible study at his home with other members from his church. I did, and met some very nice people. Weeks into the Bible Study, however, I started to see that their belief concerning faith versus baptism was different than what I understood God's Word to say. They taught that water baptism, not faith, was essential to your salvation: "Therefore being justified by *faith*, we have peace with God through our Lord Jesus Christ" (Romans 10:9; Ephesians 2:8-9; John 3:16 & 36; 5:24; Acts 16:31; Romans 3:22-26; 5:1; Galatians 3:14, 22, 24; Philippians 3:9; 2 Timothy 3:15). This was a red flag.

I had given my life to Christ as a young child but wanted to renew my commitment to God. I also wanted to be baptized again because I hoped this baptism would *finally* "wash away the gay."

It was January and Los Angeles was experiencing high winds and unusually cold temperatures on the night of my baptism. The baptism would be held outside. I was already recovering from the flu bug that was hitting everyone particularly hard that winter so I feared getting out of the water with a wet head. I sat in the car and prayed for God to protect me from the elements. People arrived from the church, along with some of my friends, and we made our way outside where the baptism would be performed.

A few words were said by a church elder before I was immersed in the water. When I came out of the water, I noticed I was warmer than I expected but didn't think much about it. I walked inside, changed into dry clothes, and made my way back outside again. It was very cold and the wind was blowing. I tried not to panic at the thought of getting sick again.

After everyone left, one of my friends asked if I had noticed what happened with the weather. She said that before the baptism was performed, the wind stopped but when I went inside to change out of my wet clothes, the wind picked back up. That unexpected gift from God really meant a lot to me.

The next day I posted on Facebook that I had given my life to Christ. Many sent supportive messages but I noticed that the majority of my "worldly" friends, even gay friends, were silent. I knew I was about to find myself with fewer friends.

When he saw my post, a pastor from another church reached out with a supportive email message. I briefly told him about the new church I had been attending. He asked what the name of the church was. When I told him he said he believed this church might be a cult, forwarded a link with additional information, and asked that I keep an open mind. I trusted he was motivated by concern for me.

I spent several days on the Internet researching everything I could about this worldwide church organization. My heart sank when I found quite a bit of information from former members who detailed serious issues including harassment, use of guilt, manipulation, even isolation from family members.

Once I moved past the shock of the information I found, I knew I could not, in good conscience, continue attending or invite other people to this church. The upside was it forced me to delve into God's Word to understand what scripture had to say about faith versus baptism. Whether it was actually a cult or not, I decided to break away from that particular church.

# 19. Nobody Puts ~~baby~~ Jesus in a Corner!

There are testimonies from Jews who share their disbelief as to why rabbis never shared with them the fifty-third chapter of the Old Testament book of Isaiah, which provides clues about the identity of the Messiah. Jewish prophets, under divine inspiration by the Holy Spirit, spoke of a worldwide impact of a Jewish Messiah (Isaiah 49:60).

*The Gospel of Matthew*, who was Jewish, confirmed Jesus' genealogy and fulfillment of the Old Testament prophecies proving He was the long-awaited Messiah. Jesus is the only person in history who met *all* of the qualifications. The Bible stresses the importance of genealogy for the Jewish people because the genealogies outline the familial scope of God's plan of salvation.

In Luke 24:44, Jesus declared He was the Messiah. If Jesus' claims had been false, there was no better time for the religious leaders to have offered a reward for Jesus' body after the Resurrection to prove Jesus was a liar, a fraud, and a nutcase. But they couldn't. It is a historical fact that hundreds of people saw Jesus alive and walking around *after* His resurrection.

What sets Jesus apart from all other prophets, gurus, yogis, ascended masters, even charlatans who claimed to be the Messiah, is that Jesus is God's only begotten Son. He was also virgin born. The others did not live a sinless life. Jesus did. They did not die for our salvation. Jesus did. They could not promise us eternal life. Jesus does. They did not cheat death. Jesus was the only one who

defeated death after having been buried *three days* in a tomb
(Matthew 28; John 20; 1 Corinthians 15).

Some of Jesus' followers, who were with Jesus before His
death *and* after His resurrection, died horrible deaths. They
refused to renounce their faith. The Apostle Paul, a religious
Pharisee who knew the law and was instrumental in persecuting
Christians, eventually came to the knowledge that Jesus is who He
claimed to be. Paul surrendered his life to Christ and preached the
Gospel. As a result, he was whipped with thirty-nine lashes on five
different occasions, stoned and survived, beaten with rods on
three different occasions, and imprisoned (2 Corinthians 11).
People will not suffer and die for something they know to be a lie.

God declares us all to be sinners (Romans 3:10 & 23;
Ecclesiastes 7:20; Isaiah 64:6), which means, "to miss the mark of
God's holy standard of righteousness." While some will be
offended by that statement, as most of us feel we are good people,
I came to see that we must put ourselves under God's microscope
and look at this matter from His perspective. We are being judged
by *His* perfect standard. Though we sin and come short of the
Glory of God, we are justified before God because Jesus was willing
to become the redemption price for man's sin. Every sinner may
come to Jesus to freely receive full pardon and forgiveness because
of His atoning work (Hebrews 9:11-14, 23-28). This is what sets
Christianity apart from all other religions in that Jesus did the
work for us (John 10:9; John 14:6; Acts 4:12; Ephesians 2:18;

Hebrews 12:2). Other religions are going to insist that *you* do the work for salvation, which is impossible.

If there were other ways to God other than through Jesus, then He would be the worst God of all because what parent would put their child on a cross to die for mankind and then tell the world they could come another way? The suffering and death of that child would be in vain. From a logical standpoint we would declare that parent insane.

Jesus wasn't a robot without feelings. To truly appreciate what Jesus did *for us*, please read the recorded accounts of the brutality that Jesus suffered in the following chapters: Matthew 26, 27; Mark 14, 15; Luke 22, 23; and John 18, 19. You can also Google search "*A Physician's View of the Crucifixion of Jesus Christ*" to understand what His body endured from a medical perspective.

It's unfortunate many believe the lie that God is angry, vengeful, and out to get us when we mess up. God does care about us: "For I know the thoughts that I think toward you, says the Lord, thoughts of peace, and not of evil, to give you an expected end. Then shall you call upon me, and you shall go and pray unto me, and I will hearken unto you. And you shall seek me, and find me, when you shall search for me with all your heart" (Jeremiah 29:11-13).

God has better things to do than to make up silly stories and fairy tales about salvation, Heaven, and Hell. God's plan is for our benefit but *the way* we must come is through His Son, Jesus. The explanation as to *why* has been outlined.

# 20. Could It Be...Satan?
## (From the Mouths of Satanists)

The Bible speaks of Satan as a real being, with the fallen angels as his agents, often referred to as demons (Isaiah 14:12-15; Luke 4:41; 10:18; James 2:19). They use violence and deceit, inflict disease, even possess people. This foe is not to be taken lightly. The lunacy of Satan and his schemes is that he has convinced most of humanity that he does not exist. However, he implicates himself as a liar and exposes his true colors by leading his followers down a path of destruction by convincing them to renounce Christ and blaspheme the Holy Spirit. Why?

The Holy Spirit works to lead us to the truth and knowledge of Jesus Christ (John 16:13). I learned that when an individual continues to resist giving his or her life to Christ, the danger is that the individual's heart and conscience will eventually become so calloused that he or she will no longer feel the striving of the Holy Spirit. That's why we should never delay accepting Christ as our Savior when feeling led by the Holy Spirit. Satan's wish is that we continue to delay our decision until it's too late. Behind the scenes, in the spiritual realm, there is a battle being waged between God and Satan for *your* soul (Ephesians 6:11-13).

Sadly, pastors in many churches have stopped extending an invitation to accept Jesus as their Savior at the end of a worship service. If the power of the Holy Spirit is moving in someone's life, and that individual feels led to give their life to Christ, the opportunity needs to be given to them. That individual should *immediately* be counseled and guided in prayer to receive Jesus Christ as their Savior *at that very moment.* Souls are at stake and tomorrow is not guaranteed for any of us.

There are Satanists who try to discredit God by taking scripture out of context, even encouraging people to blaspheme the Holy Spirit. It is stressed that their blasphemy be unquestionably premeditated and deliberate. The renunciation of the Trinity should be written in their words and should be venomous and utterly demeaning. They must take full responsibility for their blasphemy in sight of both "God" (their quotes) and Satan. It was also suggested they perform a sacrilegious gesture against some symbol of Christianity.

One traditional gesture is to put a Christian symbol on the floor and stomp on it, or place the symbol in a dish and spit on it, or even urinate or defecate on it. It was also suggested to use ripped-out pages of the Bible as toilet paper. Some might have Crosses tattooed on the soles of the feet so that the symbol of Christ is continually trodden underfoot. The physical desecration of a Christian symbol is not essential to the rite. What *is* essential is the blasphemy itself *plus* the premeditation.

Some Satanists confirm getting their tenets directly from Satan himself and believe they can "save" their own souls as opposed to the claims of the "Nazarene" saving anyone. Nazarene is a condescending reference to Jesus, who was a Nazarene.

An Atheist group organized a blasphemy challenge and encouraged people to blaspheme the Holy Spirit on video and post them on social networking websites.

If God doesn't exist then why are these people spending time mocking Jesus and encouraging people to blaspheme the Holy Spirit? Why isn't the same effort and venom being spewed toward other religions? The bottom line is that the *influence* is demonic. Satan knows his only threat is Jesus. When exorcisms are performed, it is a fact that only one name can be used to deliver those under demonic possession and that name is *Jesus*. Demons must submit and obey the authority of Jesus.

There are websites and YouTube videos from former witches alleging that Harry Potter books promote witchcraft and desensitize children to the dangers of the occult world. Children will find that seeing "ghosts and dark entities" as normal, unaware that rituals and casting spells open demonic portals. There is no such thing as "white magic." God denounces all forms of occult practice (Leviticus 19:26 & 31; 20:6; Deuteronomy 18:12; Galatians 5:20) and warns that those who do these things "shall not inherit the kingdom of God" (Galatians 5:21). God is not giving these warnings because He's a cruel dictator. Just like any loving parent who wants to protect their child from danger, God is warning us because He knows these are strategies of Satan to deceive, harm, and destroy us (John 10:10; 1 Peter 5:8).

Jesus didn't mince words when He exposed Satan for who he is: "...he was a murderer from the beginning, and abode not in the truth, because there is no truth in him...for he is a liar, and the father of it" (John 8:44).

Some have argued that since religion is the cause of wars and human suffering, they want nothing to do with God. They are unable to see that religion has nothing to do with God. Some believe that Satan is co-equal with God but this is not the case. Satan is not omnipresent, omniscient, or omnipotent. Satan is a created being (by God) with limited power. Some have stated that since God created Satan then He created evil. Not so. Just like we have a choice to obey or disobey God, Satan *chose* to rebel against God. God gives mankind *free will*, which means He allows us to choose to do good or evil, to sin, or to turn from sin. God makes it clear I am responsible for my actions and behavior so I cannot blame Him or anyone else for my sin.

Jesus' death and resurrection was the final blow to Satan. Satan thought he had won the game by having Jesus nailed to the Cross. Little did Satan know that he was just a pawn in the Eternal Plan of God to accomplish salvation for all men who would believe in Jesus, trusting Him to save them. Satan unwittingly helped fulfill the prophecy that required Jesus dying as a sacrifice. Jesus' shed blood and death on the Cross helped sinful mankind escape the grip of Satan (1 Peter 1:18-21). Satan's victory was really God's victory. Death couldn't even hold Jesus in the grave. Since Satan is not omniscient, he had no idea about the *eternal* plan of redemption for mankind.

Satan and all demonic forces have been defeated. God warns in Revelation 20:10 (future prophecy): "And the devil that deceived them was cast into the lake of fire and brimstone, where the beast and the false prophet are, and shall be tormented day and night for ever and ever." Satan and his angels live with this knowledge every day, unable to undo their mistake.

# 21. The Power of Christ Compels You!

One night I stumbled upon a YouTube video by Pastor Derek Prince.  He spoke about demonic bondage (Acts 5:16; Matthew 8:28; Ephesians 6:11-13) and generational curses (Number 14:18).  I took a deeper look at these subjects because I couldn't understand why I continued to struggle with a same-sex attraction, depression, and thoughts of suicide.  Were demons the root cause of my same-sex attraction?  I learned Christians can't be possessed by demons because possession implies ownership and we have been bought with the blood of Jesus Christ.  However, we can be oppressed or in bondage due to doorways we open, essentially giving demons the legal right to enter.  One area is lack of forgiveness:

> "For if you forgive men their trespasses, your Heavenly Father will also forgive you.  But if you forgive not men their trespasses, neither will your Father forgive your trespasses" (Matthew 6:14-15; also 18:21-22; John 15:17; Ephesians 4:32).

Pastors who specialize in demonic deliverance will not move forward in helping an individual until they have truly forgiven those who hurt them.

One night, as I was taking a walk, God revealed my lack of forgiveness toward Christians.  I had been so focused on forgiving specific people that I didn't think about the contempt I felt about the Christian community as a whole.  It pained me to think about toxic Christians who convinced me God hated me because I was a homosexual.  That's why I was always so torn in my relationship with God and would draw close to Him only to turn and run.  I expected God to reject me just like other people had in the past.

God understands forgiveness can be a slow process.  I came to see that I must continually ask God to help me forgive an individual until the matter is settled peacefully in my heart.  Forgiveness is important to the Lord.  While Jesus was being crucified, He prayed for His enemies (Luke 23:34).

I eventually reached out to Shannon Davis, host of Omegaman Radio, who specialized in demonic deliverance and he recommended a pastor in my area.  One Sunday morning I drove to Malibu and visited the church.  I decided I was going to cover all the bases.  I nervously sat in the small church saying "hello" to the people who extended a warm greeting.  As I was hoping to be exorcised of a gay demon, I couldn't help but notice a cute guy sitting on the other side of the church.  To the *Carrie* movie fans, cue Piper Laurie's voice:  *"Eve was weak.  Sin never dies!"*

After the service, the pastor began a mass deliverance prayer.  I didn't know what to expect as I'd heard the process is different for each individual.  As the pastor led the congregation, I could hear people moaning, growling, some were making strange sounds, and women were screaming.  It was unsettling, but I focused on my prayer to God and agreed with what the pastor said.  At the end, a woman put her hand on my back and asked if she could pray with me.  I told her how I was struggling with a same-sex attraction, depression, and suicidal thoughts.  She prayed and I started sobbing.  After a long prayer session with her, the pastor also prayed one-on-one with me. I left the church and decided I would try another session the following week.

For some, deliverance may take time due to numerous areas that needed to be addressed. I had initially been under the impression that deliverance happens immediately and all of your problems "magically" disappear.

At the next service I attended, a man put his hand on my back as I was praying with the pastor after the service. Once again, during the prayer people coughed, spit stuff up, screamed, cried, and growled while I stayed calm and focused. As the man prayed with me, I started sobbing and begged God for deliverance. The man started speaking in tongues, a gift that allows certain people to speak in an unknown language while communicating or praising God (1 Corinthians 14:2; Acts 10:46).

There's no way to tell if this actually freed me from demonic bondage but I knew I felt much "lighter." This may seem extreme to some but when you're desperate for peace of mind, you will do anything, and everything, for relief. I *was* desperate. So, had I been delivered? I was still attracted to guys but perhaps I had gotten rid of some of those demons. I didn't return for any more deliverance.

# 22. Sodom and Gomorrah

As a young man, I dreaded reading any passages concerning Sodom and Gomorrah in the Bible. Real peace and freedom came, however, when I faced that fear and started studying God's Word. I have no agenda in the information being presented because, for the record, I have a healthy fear, reverence, and respect for God. I would never twist God's Word to fit my selfish desires.

In one of the most disturbing passages of Scripture, Judges 19, it details a man and his concubine visiting a place called Gibeah. Hospitality was very important back then and visitors often had to rely upon the kindness of strangers for food and lodging. A local resident kindly offered them a place to stay. A group of men gathered at the door demanding that the master of the house "bring forth the man that came into thine house, that we may know him" (verse 22). To "know" meant to know him sexually. The man of the house begged them not to do something so wicked and, instead, offered his daughter or his guest, the concubine. Well the concubine was pushed outside and the men "knew her and abused her all night long."

The homosexual men I know wouldn't have had sex with that woman. The drag queens would have stolen her purse, dress, and high-heeled shoes. If she was wearing a dated hairstyle, the gay hairdressers would have cut, highlighted, and teased her hair. Common sense would suggest this wasn't about homosexuality as much as it was a bunch of brutes looking to humiliate and degrade an individual, like they do in prison.

Regarding Sodom and Gomorrah in Genesis 19, it states that two angels (disguised as men) arrived in Sodom. Lot graciously offered the men a place to stay because that was the thing to do...be hospitable. In Genesis 19:4-8, the men of the city were not only being inhospitable, but they wanted to engage in gang rape of the male visitors. Lot pleaded with them not to do something so wicked and offered his two daughters instead. Common sense begs this question. All the years Lot spent in Sodom, was he unable to comprehend that offering females to a group of homosexual men was the most asinine offer he could make?

In Genesis 18, three angels, who were in human form, appeared to Abraham. God was planning on destroying these cities *before* the incident with Lot ever happened. We know this because in verse 23 Abraham asked God if He would destroy the righteous with the wicked. Abraham then asked if He would spare the city if 50 righteous people could be found. God agreed to spare the city. Then Abraham proceeded to ask if He would spare the city if just 45, then 40, then 30, then 20, and finally 10 righteous people could be found. Yes, the city would be spared. So Sodom would have been spared if they found just ten righteous people. Sounds like a fair and loving God to me!

So what were the sins of Sodom and Gomorrah? The only thing we are told in Genesis 18:20 is that "their sin is very grievous." Sodom and Gomorrah were often cited as warnings to *other* cities that were about to be destroyed because of their sin and wickedness. I encourage you to read the following passages in the Bible for yourself.

In Isaiah, Chapters 1, 2, 3 and 13, addressing Judah, Jerusalem and Babylon: Murder, oppression, neglect of orphans and widows, corrupt, companion of thieves, rebellious, idolatry, haughty, proud, greedy, women tempted men with lust.

Jeremiah 23, addressing Judah: Adulterers, liars, corrupt religious leaders, poor shepherding, unfaithful to God, godless priests and prophets, condoned wickedness, do what you want - God is okay with it, prophesied lies in God's name.

Jeremiah 49, addressing Edom: Lack of wisdom, loss of reasoning, neglect of widows and children, pride.

Jeremiah 50, addressing Babylon: Idolatry, prideful, liars, oppression of children.

Lamentations 4, addressing Zion (Jerusalem): Impurity, loss of maternal instinct, child neglect (mothers are compared to ostriches who lay their eggs and then neglect them), child abuse, cannibalism, bloodshed.

Ezekiel 16, addressing Jerusalem. God speaks of her as a prostitute: Immoral, idolatry, child sacrifice, arrogant, adultery, lack of concern for the poor and needy.

Amos 4, addressing Israel: Idolatry, the rich oppressed the poor, sacrifices that did not please God.

In Matthew 10:14-15 (also Mark 6:11; Luke 10:11-12), Sodom and Gomorrah are mentioned but it was due to hospitality. Jesus told the disciples to go and preach the Gospel. If a city did not receive them, refusing to hear their words, they were told to "shake the dust off their feet" and that "It shall be more tolerable for the land of Sodom and Gomorrah in the day of judgment, than for that city."

> 2 Peter 2, addressing churches in Asia Minor (modern-day Turkey): False prophets and teachers, filthy conversation, wickedness, lawless, lust.

> Jude 1, addressing churches: Lasciviousness, false prophets, fornication, going after strange flesh (sex with angels), lust.

How unfortunate that homosexuality has been relegated to the "worst of all sins" by many Christians.

Romans 1:26-28 is another passage of scripture often used to condemn homosexuals:

> "For this cause God gave them up unto vile affections: for even their women did change the natural use into that which is against nature: And likewise also the men, leaving the natural use of the woman, burned in their lust one toward another; men with men working that which is unseemly, and receiving in themselves that recompense of their error which was meet. And even as they did not like to retain God in their knowledge, God gave them over to a reprobate mind, to do those things which are not convenient (i.e. fitting or becoming)."

Clearly, this passage of scripture is dealing with heterosexual women and men who were so depraved they began to engage in homosexual acts. Homosexuals and heterosexuals can be consumed with lust just as there are heterosexuals and homosexuals who seek monogamous relationships.

Also, the term "reprobate mind" has always made me cringe. I associated it with the mind of a homosexual. I searched the Internet, including several Christian websites, for definitions of a "reprobate mind" and this is what I found:

> "Unprincipled (not acting in accordance with moral principles), godless, wicked, corrupt, all light removed from them, rejected by God and beyond hope of salvation, morally depraved, disobedient, abominable, someone who has rejected the Faith,

someone who has gone so far in rejection and sin that he or she is unmoved by the Holy Spirit, someone who has no head, no hunger, no heart for God and His work and His will for their life, insensitive and unmoved by the Gospel."

While I'm not perfect, according to this definition I don't have a "reprobate mind." I *do* agonize over my relationship with God, have a heart for God, and a strong desire to please Him.

Some within the LGBT community have been falsely led to believe Sodom and Gomorrah were destroyed simply because of a "hospitality" issue. Since when has the world ever been hospitable? If this was the sole reason for God destroying these two cities, why hasn't this planet been annihilated?

Let's get real. Homosexuality, especially the attempted rape of angels, was a primary factor. However, the destruction of Sodom and Gomorrah was because of *all* sin and wickedness before God. There has never been an all-heterosexual, sinless society.

The Bible is not meant to abuse people. God doesn't have an ax to grind with homosexuals. God is not homophobic. He doesn't hate the LGBT community. God's issue is with *sin*...the sin of homosexuals *and* heterosexuals.

# 23. Hollywood Nights

There were years I didn't struggle with my faith and sexuality simply because I was mentally and emotionally exhausted from dealing with it all the time. I stopped caring and stopped going to church. God took a back seat to finding love. In spite of numerous one-night stands, I always hoped I would find a man who would be faithful and love me the way I desired to be loved. I wanted the security of a home and someone to grow old with.

It was the late-1990's when I was introduced to something called "The Internet." Alanis Morissette and Nirvana dominated the local radio stations. America Online (AOL) was all the rage because of the Internet chat rooms. I would search for M4M (male for male) chat rooms and chat with guys. It was a quick and easy way to meet guys and eventually hook-up for dates and/or sex. While most of my sexual encounters were with gay men, some were bisexual or "curious" and wanted to experiment with a guy. I met many heterosexual men who were married or had girlfriends and complained about their sex lives; they didn't feel it was cheating if it was with another guy. I didn't care. Sexually satisfying a straight guy seemed like a way to compensate for not being accepted by the straight boys in school. My self-worth was completely tied to sex. Outside of sex I felt I had nothing to offer anyone.

A few of my encounters were not so pleasant. One afternoon, I invited a guy to my apartment. We started kissing and removing our clothes. Suddenly, he became aggressive, pinned me face down on the floor, and sexually assaulted me. I was in pain and struggled but couldn't break free from his grip. It happened so fast and he left. In the days that followed, he would leave threatening voicemail messages saying he was going to return and slit my throat. I was scared to go home alone and would often enter my apartment holding a knife in my hand for fear he might be hiding somewhere inside. I never called the police because I didn't think they would believe me. Thankfully, after about a week, the harassment ceased.

Because he didn't use protection, I worried about HIV. I made an appointment with the LGBT clinic in Hollywood and went in for an HIV test. I was terrified waiting for the results. When the counselor told me I was "negative," it was such a relief that I started sobbing. Exiting the office, other people in the waiting room saw my red swollen face and watery eyes, probably assuming I received a "positive" read. I couldn't exit the building fast enough because I was so relieved.

I spoke with a number of straight men in chat rooms who wanted to experiment with a guy but only if he was dressed as a female so, for a brief time, I experimented with cross-dressing. I purchased wigs, fishnet stockings, makeup, lingerie or whatever it took to fulfill someone's fantasy. It was a desperate attempt to feel desired, loved, and wanted by a man, even if it was only temporary. I loved being with straight guys. What must it be like for a woman to have a guy fawn all over her, want to take care of her, and protect her? I was obviously tapping into some deeper issues of being bullied and wishing I had a strong man to protect me.

The downside was that some guys seemed incapable of separating fantasy from reality and that led to some disturbing conversations. I envisioned a future of filing restraining orders so I stopped cross-dressing.

I heard plenty of other dating and hook-up horror stories from friends and acquaintances. It didn't matter. Even when a friend of mine was murdered by a stranger he had met and invited into his home, I didn't heed the warnings. I was searching for love.

I started talking to another guy on the Internet and, after several pleasant conversations, we agreed to meet. Stephan was an attractive brunette with a lean body. We spent a couple of months hanging out and "fooling around." On our way to dinner one evening, he made it clear we were not a couple. He said he was bisexual and enjoyed sex with women. I was stunned and hurt, but things finally started to make sense. Whenever it was time to sleep, he would go to his own bedroom instead of us sleeping together and cuddling. Maybe he was struggling with his sexuality. I had already developed deep feelings for him and it was difficult sleeping alone knowing he was nearby. I clung to the hope he would fall in love with me and stop desiring women.

I would often lie in bed at night and cry. The emotional pain became so intense that I imagined going to the kitchen, getting a knife, and slitting my wrists. I actually thought that as the blood drained from my veins the pain would leave as well. I eventually found the courage to walk away from him when I finally accepted our situation was never going to change.

Not long after, I met a Latin guy on a dating website and, after chatting, agreed to meet him for coffee in Hollywood. We hit it off and I often hung out at his place. We took things slowly for the first month since I wasn't ready to rush into anything. Our time together was very innocent with us just hanging out, going to dinner, or lying in bed and watching movies before falling asleep in each other's arms.

About six weeks into our relationship, my feelings for Luis had developed. However, after what I had been through with Stephan, I had learned to ask questions. I asked Luis if he had ever been with a woman or if he considered himself bisexual. To my surprise he not only said "yes" but told me he had an ex-girlfriend that he occasionally visited for sex. While I appreciated his honesty, I wasn't going through that again and abruptly ended it. I had learned my lesson.

I met a guy on the Internet with blue eyes and blond hair. He seemed like a decent guy and we dated for four months. Little did I know Donald was sleeping around on me the whole time. His friends, who liked me but wanted to stay loyal to their friend, kept trying to warn me in a roundabout way. I was just too stupid to get it. Why would someone do that to another person? When I finally found out, it took months for me to recover from the devastation of the betrayal.

I was eventually ready to date again and met Liam on the Internet. We agreed to have dinner in West Hollywood. He was an attractive, slender brunette and I looked forward to our evening together. Once seated at the restaurant, we started with small talk until he disclosed that he was an actor in porn films. I wasn't necessarily shocked by what he did, as I knew several guys who starred in porn films, but it was disappointing because I was getting exhausted and frustrated with the dating scene.

After dinner, we walked to his apartment. Liam wanted to watch one of his porn tapes but I politely ended the date. I was feeling down and discouraged. I really wanted a relationship with a stable man who had the same relationship goals I had. Why was it so hard to find true love? I decided to put men and dating on the backburner and remain celibate. I was tired of having my heart broken. This turned out to be one of the best decisions I ever made because it allowed time for some emotional healing.

On a trip to Istanbul, Turkey, an employee of the hotel where I was staying caught my eye in the hallway. He focused his stare on me and I nodded. He watched me go into my room. As I was cleaning up, there was a knock at the door and it was the employee. I invited him in.

We briefly chatted and then removed our clothes and kissed. He suddenly became aggressive and positioned me in a way where I couldn't move. After the sexual assault, I was in pain and bleeding. I was in tears as the fear of HIV flooded my mind again. When I returned to Los Angeles, I went in for another HIV test and, thankfully, it came back *negative.*

The emptiness and loneliness I felt led me back to the clubs and bars. Sometimes I just needed to be around guys. If I happened to meet someone I was attracted to and sex came into play, so be it. I had given up on celibacy as I missed being with a guy.

One night, I drove to a small, dive bar on a quiet street outside of Hollywood. It was a place I visited often. I exited my car and slowly walked into the dimly lit bar while industrial music pulsated through the speakers. It was so dark inside that you couldn't see faces but you could see the shadowy figures of guys lined up against the walls. If any sexual activity was happening, I couldn't tell. I would find a spot along the wall and stay focused on the more well-lit area where guys in leather were walking around.

One night I approached an attractive guy in full leather regalia, which consisted of boots, pants, cap, and straps across his chiseled, worked-out, shirtless chest. I was curious about the "leather scene" and what that entailed. While I asked purely out of curiosity, the guy was clearly not in the mood for a Barbara Walters interview and quickly let me know that he wanted to take me back to his place. After he detailed his slave (me) / master (him) fantasy, I told him I wasn't interested. He became aggressive and started swearing at me. I left the bar.

Down the street from the leather bar was a sex club. After you paid a small fee, they handed you condoms as you entered the club. I decided to check it out. I walked in the door and to my right I noticed a blindfolded guy tied to what looked like a hammock/sling used in sadism and masochism (S&M) bondage scenes. He was positioned and ready for any guy who wanted to use him for sex. I was quite shocked at first then decided to cruise the rest of the joint.

The place was a maze of both dark and well-lit rooms used for anonymous sex. I had no idea men were waiting in the shadows when entering a dark room. Several hands were on me and my clothes were being removed. Panic set in. I feared being sexually assaulted and catching HIV. I struggled to keep my clothes on while pushing men off of me. I managed to exit the room and left the club.

Some nights I didn't feel like dealing with the pretentiousness of the West Hollywood club scene so I'd visit a known hustler bar in Hollywood. Sometimes rich, older men would offer to pay for time with younger guys. There was nothing glamorous about this bar or the neighborhood location. It was common to see prostitutes roaming the streets. When you entered, the bar was to the right and had bowls of popcorn waiting for the patrons. There were a couple of pinball machines in the front and pool tables in the back. On the left side of the bar was the jukebox along with an assortment of tables where people could sit and chat.

I met everyone from drag queens to male and female prostitutes, even runaways (some of whom were kicked out of homes and disowned by family members simply because they were gay). I met a guy who had just gotten out of prison while old men drank until they passed out at the bar. Fag hags (straight women who spend most of their time with gay guys) and gay men danced and sang to the music that played on the jukebox. Many of these people were down on their luck. Through the years I heard heartbreaking stories, as many of them were open and honest about their lives. But no matter how cruel life had been to them, they were a breath of fresh air because they were real. I would often sit and watch the crowd and my heart would ache. Sometimes I imagined Jesus walking into the bar and showing nothing but love and compassion for the people inside.

The dichotomy of how people live in Los Angeles really hit me one night when I walked into an upscale restaurant on Melrose Avenue in West Hollywood. I had the pleasure of meeting and having a friendly conversation with a well-known actor who was dining in a private booth. After dinner, I drove to a convenience store to pick up a few items only to find several homeless people outside begging for money to buy food. As I purchased a few hot dogs for the homeless people, I watched a limousine pull into the parking lot while the passenger exited the vehicle to purchase a pack of cigarettes. To see all of this within a one-hour period was jolting. It was hard to digest the sad reality of those who have so much living next to those who have nothing at all.

Life in the City of Angels was certainly interesting.  It had the beauty, the mansions, the ocean, the snow-capped mountains, palm trees, the celebrities, even the view of the dazzling city lights at night from the Hollywood Hills.  In spite of all its charms, the city was also filled with people who were broken, whose dreams never came true, who were searching for something they would never find in material possessions, money, fame, endless sexual encounters, drugs, or the bottle.  I often felt alone and empty.  I wasn't finding the utopia I thought I would find at the end of the gay rainbow.  I realized I couldn't live my life this way any longer. Something had to change.

# 24. At the Reflection Pond

I wonder what my life would be like today if I had grown up having a safe place to share my struggle with Christians. I never thought of God as my ally. Sadly, I chose a path of self-destruction and made some very poor choices. I can't go back and change it. What's done is done and I accept full responsibility for all of it. However, my painful journey helped me learn some things about myself *and* about God. I am grateful for what I've been through. My struggles helped me to understand God's grace and mercy on a deeper level. I am lucky to be alive and thankful that He gave me a second chance.

I had to stop fighting God. When I *truly surrendered to His will*, not my will, I noticed a change happening in my life. This sent me on a journey in which God had to "clean house," deprogram my mind of the lies I absorbed about Him from toxic Christians, and open my eyes to the deception of the homosexual lifestyle.

I didn't realize that freedom from my former life wouldn't happen overnight. It would take a committed relationship with God to find true liberation. God already had all the facts and understood my deep-rooted hurts, fears, trauma, and insecurities. He knew what drove the unhealthy behavioral and thought patterns that kept me in bondage. He knew what it would take for me to get the right kind of healing. I naively thought if the right guy came along, the void would be filled and the pain would go away.

For many of us, the need for love and affection can be just as addictive as drugs and alcohol.  I desperately wanted and craved love from a male figure.  When my father and I would have heart-to-heart conversations about this subject and "coming out of the homosexual lifestyle," my emotions ranged from rage to hurt.  I thought my father didn't understand what he was asking of his son.  I couldn't imagine living life without having someone to love.

It's easy for a Christian to tell a homosexual they need to leave the homosexual lifestyle without putting themselves in the shoes of the individual.

Imagine God issuing a decree that heterosexuality was now wrong under all circumstances and that homosexuality was His divine plan.  You must now leave the love of your life and force yourself to be intimate with someone of the same sex.  As disgusting as that is to think about, you either obey God or choose a lifelong path of celibacy and loneliness.  Then you come to me, crying, explaining you can't force yourself to have feelings for someone of the same sex, that the thought of same-sex intimacy nauseates you.  You are depressed and/or suicidal but I so coldly respond with: *"You don't want to change.  You love your sin too much.  You don't want to please God."*  Then I tell you that the church will not provide a class where you can find others struggling with heterosexuality.  This is how it feels for an individual who is truly struggling with a same-sex attraction!

We are expected to walk an excruciatingly lonely path while the majority of churches are unwilling to provide a support system for homosexuals looking to escape that life. I feared leaving "that life" because I feared losing my only support system. In a world filled with LGBT individuals, I didn't feel like an outsider. I felt like I finally belonged somewhere.

Understand that when we leave the LGBT life, most of our friends abandon us. Many radical activists attack us for daring to share our stories. It goes against the narrative that *change is impossible* so we must be silenced. Without a Christian support system, many will return to that life or struggle with isolation, depression, and despair.

Love is a powerful force. My desire for love and affection was equally as strong as my desire to have a relationship with God. To be told a same-sex relationship and a relationship with God are at odds with each other and that you must choose between the two is devastating. Whatever decision is made, something must be sacrificed which is why I struggled for so long with depression.

At times the road on my journey was dark and tough. I lost friends. I felt I didn't know who I was anymore and I definitely didn't know where my journey with God would take me. I was afraid of the unknown and at times God seemed distant. I wanted to run back to my old life because it was a safety net even though I knew, in my heart, that it wasn't the answer. I had no choice but to move forward.

I started with baby steps and, thankfully, God was patient. He knew healing and wholeness had to come *first* in order for me to finally have the strength to walk away from my former life. God graciously delivered me from a sexual addiction. My same-sex attraction hasn't changed but it no longer controls me. I have chosen the road of celibacy. I take it one day at a time similar to any married heterosexual male or female who struggles with lust or temptation to stray outside of his or her relationship.

While there is a cost to following Christ, the benefits and blessings far outweigh it. The cost is nothing compared to what Jesus endured for me (for all of us) on the Cross.

The most surprising part of this journey is that the more God revealed His true nature to me, drawing me closer to Him, the more my love for Him grew. I willingly serve Him and have no regrets about giving my life to Christ. That's why I remain committed to God in spite of my unfortunate experience with some members of the Christian community.

My hope is that Christians will extend compassion to a community who need to hear about the forgiveness and hope that is available in Christ, and that there is a Savior who loves them and died for all of us.

I lived approximately twenty-five years in a life that was filled with sex, drugs, alcohol, and other worldly pleasures but, at the end of the day, I felt empty. There was a constant void and an ache those things could never fill. I didn't have peace of mind or peace with God because I was under conviction. As hard as I tried to reconcile the arguments in favor of homosexuality, even same-sex marriage, I could not, in good conscience, ignore God's truth any longer.

- God first created...male and female (Genesis 2:21-23; Matthew 19:4).

- God gives a blueprint for marriage. It is a divine institution, a covenant marriage relationship before God between a man and a woman, not someone of the same sex (Genesis 2:24; Matthew 19:5-6).

- Sexual intimacy is designed to be between husband and wife. Therefore, sex (even heterosexual sex) outside of marriage is forbidden (1 Corinthians 7:2).

- Heterosexuality is a divine creation, affirmed and blessed by God, whereas God's Word speaks negatively of homosexual behavior in the Bible (Leviticus 18:22; 20:13; Romans 1:26-27; 1 Corinthians 6:9; Matthew 19:4-5).

- There are no instances recorded of a same-sex relationship or marriage in the Bible.

- God even had something to say about heterosexual marriage between a believer and an unbeliever. Although valid, God still commands us to avoid such marriages (1 Corinthians 7:14; 2 Corinthians 6:14).

- Whenever the Bible mentions marriage, fidelity is the divine intention. It speaks of a lifelong union between a man and a woman for the purpose of having a family, providing a stable environment, with instructions on how to raise Godly children (Matthew 19:4-6; Ephesians 5:23-33; 6:4; Genesis 18:19; Proverbs 13:24; 22:6; 29:17).

- The relationship between David and Jonathan is often cited as a homosexual relationship from some within the gay community. Jonathan was the son of Saul, the king of Israel, and both would eventually die in battle (1 Samuel 31). It's clear that David and Jonathan had a special bond. David confirming Jonathan's love for him as "passing the love of women" (2 Samuel 1:26) is, to me, a beautiful love story. I wish God had taken the time to define this as a homosexual relationship but God does not say this nor are we told they had sexual relations. I have relationships with males that I love and care for as much as my own family but I'm not having sex with them so I cannot presume this was a homosexual relationship. We are given some insight into David and Jonathan's relationship in 1 Samuel, chapters 18, 19, 20, and in 2 Samuel, chapter 1.

- Both men were married and fathered children.

- We see qualities of a true friendship, which involved emotions, loyalty, and sacrifice. They loved each other.

- When these two friends parted, of course it would be emotional. This had nothing to do with sex.

- When they kissed (1 Samuel 20:41), I cannot assume it was a French kiss. In some cultures, it is a common gesture to kiss each other on the cheek.

- God would not have favored a homosexual relationship between David and Jonathan, contradicting His teachings elsewhere in the Bible. God is not the author of confusion (1 Corinthians 14:33).

- It has also been argued that the Centurion and his servant, who was "sick and grievously tormented" (Matthew 8:5-13; Luke 7:1-10), had a same-sex relationship. The Centurion asked Jesus to heal his servant and Jesus graciously granted his request. We cannot conclude, because Jesus healed the servant, that it meant He was affirming a same-sex relationship. Jesus healed the sick, the blind, even those who were demon possessed. His healing had nothing to do with affirming the sinful behavior of anyone He healed. Jesus was caring and compassionate. Period.

Jesus' message was about "loving one another." If the relationship between the Centurion and his servant, and the relationship between David and Jonathan, were truly same-sex relationships, this would have provided perfect opportunities for God to affirm homosexual relationships *and* give us a biblical foundation for what they would look like. But God's Word doesn't elaborate further into these relationships so I can't presume they were homosexual lovers.

Some have argued that Jesus surrounded Himself with men and never married because He was gay and understood hatred and bigotry first-hand.  So Jesus...

- fasted for 40 days (not an easy feat!);
- faced temptation by Satan;
- hung out with the "outcasts," not giving a flip what the religious leaders thought about it;
- disobeyed the law by healing on the Sabbath, infuriating religious leaders, even exposing their hypocrisy to their faces;
- confronted the religious leaders who were trying to kill Him;
- went into the temple of God, driving out those who had turned His "house of prayer" into a "den of thieves";
- willingly faced, and endured, the terror of a brutal beating *and* a horrific crucifixion (!) but Jesus feared.....*bigotry*?

Jesus never struck me as a wimp who was afraid of anyone or anything.  Christian men hang out and fellowship all the time.  That doesn't make them, Jesus, or His apostles and disciples, homosexual.

If Jesus was a homosexual, His enemies would have wasted no time in exposing it to discredit Him because homosexuality was subject to capital punishment (Leviticus 20:13).  This would have alleviated their need to continue to try and find ways to trap Jesus in order to have Him killed.  They would have had cause to stone Him right there on the spot.  God made it clear that Jesus had no sin in His life (2 Corinthians 5:21; Hebrews 4:15).

Some argue that Jesus never spoke about homosexuality but He didn't have to.  His Jewish audience knew that this behavior was condemned whereas the Gentile community approved of it. The Apostle Paul, who spoke for Jesus, condemned it. Jesus didn't specifically speak about porn or spousal abuse but that doesn't mean He approved of it. Jesus is God in human form. Jesus didn't need to rehash, in the New Testament, what He addressed in the Old Testament.

- Jesus hung out with sinners and dishonest tax collectors but that didn't mean He approved of their sin. His goal was to reveal their sin, and bring them to repentance (Matthew 9:10-11; Luke 7:36-50; John 8:3-11; Mark 2:17; 1 Corinthians 6:8-11). Jesus expected them to have a heart change, and sin no more.

- Jesus didn't give a pass to the woman caught in adultery. While He shamed her accusers, Jesus also gave no indication that adultery was acceptable before God and, therefore, didn't condone it when He told her to "go and sin no more" (John 8).

Some argue that God created us to be homosexual and I used to believe that lie. God never sins nor does God tempt man to sin. Somewhere the choice is made to follow that lifestyle, whatever the reason. A loving God wouldn't create homosexuals and then condemn homosexual behavior. Hence, the admonition in James 1:12-15:

"Blessed is the man that endures temptation: for when he is tried, he shall receive the crown of life, which the Lord hath promised to them that love Him. Let no man say when he is tempted, I am tempted of God: for God cannot be tempted with evil, neither tempts He any man: But every man is tempted, when he is drawn away of his own lust, and enticed. Then when lust hath conceived, it brings forth sin: and sin, when it is finished, brings forth death."

Regarding the transgender issue, God doesn't make mistakes when assigning our gender:

> "Before I formed thee in the belly, I knew thee. For I know the thoughts that I think toward you, saith the Lord, thoughts of peace, and not evil, to give you an unexpected end." Jeremiah 1:5; 29:11

I encourage those struggling with gender dysphoria to listen to the countless testimonies on YouTube of former transgender individuals who expose the lies that you can change your gender. They were guinea pigs. They admit it didn't solve their problems nor did it bring about the peace they thought it would bring. They also expose the toll the hormone shots and surgeries took on their bodies.

Google the article at StandUpForTheTruth.com - *"Confronting the lies and propaganda of the transgender movement"* for more information on the health risks.

There are some Christians who believe that the New Testament (NT) trumps the Old Testament (OT) and the OT should be discarded because it is no longer relevant. Understand that the NT expands into further detail what the OT teaches. While the NT is written more for the *believer*, in how to live a life that is pleasing to God, it also provides the necessary information needed for the *unbeliever* to draw them to Christ. Jesus referenced the OT in His teachings so if the teachings of the OT were relevant to Him, they are still relevant today.

Some Christians will argue that we are now under *grace*. Since "grace" is defined as "free and unmerited favor of God," that does not give us the right to trample on God's grace and live as we please (Romans, Chapters 6 & 8; 1 Corinthians, chapters 5 & 6). One person may define *grace* as those moments when someone, unknowingly or unintentionally, falls short in their walk with God when trying to live according to His principles and a life that is pleasing to Him. Another may feel that numerous sexual encounters, viewing porn, lying, stealing, drug use, are all *okay* because, at the end of the day, we are under God's *grace*.

As Christians, we are held to a higher standard and must deny our selfish desires if they are in opposition to God's principles and guidelines as outlined in the Bible: "For if we sin willfully after that we have received the knowledge of the truth, there remains no more sacrifice for sins" (Hebrews 10:26).

A born-again believer in a same-sex relationship will not go to Hell. It's the rejection of Jesus that sends a person to Hell. However, If we confess to be a Christian but continue to engage in activities that are in direct opposition to God's Word, we must realize our Heavenly Father will discipline us severely if we refuse to listen.

> "My son, do not despise the chastening of the Lord, nor be discouraged when you are rebuked by Him. For whom the Lord loves He chastens, and scourges every son whom He receives. If you endure chastening, God deals with you as with sons; for what son is there whom a father does not chasten? But if you are without chastening...then you are illegitimate and not sons" (Hebrews 12:5-8).

God's Word is clear. If we are not chastened for our disobedience then we are not His children. God is a God of love but His wrath equals the depth of His love.

God does not condemn individuals because they're homosexual but an individual cannot cling to his or her sin *and* Christ at the same time. We must make a choice. *Condemnation comes as a result of rejecting Christ.*

As for the SCOTUS ruling on same-sex marriage, I believe God is pleased when we, as a society, evolve and are respectful, loving, and kind to one another. But, with this ruling, we still have to be mindful that although society changes, God never changes. Hebrews 13:8 declares that Jesus is "the same yesterday, and today, and forever." Laws enacted by our government do not trump God's laws if they are in direct opposition to His Word.

In 1 Corinthians 6:9-11, the Apostle Paul listed those who would not inherit the kingdom of God: "...neither fornicators, idolaters, adulterers, effeminate, thieves, drunkards, etc....such *were* some of you..." meaning change is possible (also Galatians 5:16-26; 6:8; Ephesians 4:19-32; 5:1-18; 1 Thessalonians 4:2-5, 7). If we have truly been saved and love God, we will desire to live a life that is pleasing to Him. "If you love me, keep my commandments" (John 14:15 & 23). There should be a change in us.

A distinction needs to be made between "homosexuality" (an attraction, which is blameless) and "homosexual behavior" (an action, which is sinful). I can't let feelings override God's truth. Facts don't care about my feelings. The heart will lead us astray.

God's Word leads us *to* Him.  True repentance is living a life for God and turning away from what God's Word defines as sin, one of which is homosexuality.  When we choose to remain in what God declares "sin," we are removing God from His throne and His rightful place in our lives and putting ourselves on that throne.  Our thoughts and desires become more important than God's.  It is rebellion against God.

Christian *allies* of the LGBT community may feel they are being a "good Christian" by supporting and affirming this "lifestyle."  While we should have the heart of Christ by loving and treating everyone with compassion and respect, encouraging a homosexual to remain in this life is encouraging further enslavement into a life that is in rebellion to God.  Jesus loved the outcasts but, still, He did not condone sin.  **Your affirmation is hurting the homosexual/transgender individual!**  They need to know deliverance is possible.  It's not about us.  It's about Jesus for He said to His disciples:

> "If any man will come after Me, let him deny himself, and take up his cross, and follow Me.  For whosoever will save his life shall lose it, and whosoever will lose his life for My sake, shall find it" (Matthew 16:24-26).

You only see the sanitized, glamorized version that Hollywood and the media portray.  There are countless testimonies on YouTube of former LGBT individuals sharing the misery of that life, what they endured, and what God did to get them *out* of that life.  You'll hear the reality of depression, low self-esteem, various addictions, prostitution, and the casualties from AIDS, murder, suicide, and drug overdoses.

When I accepted that homosexuality was not part of God's original plan, I had an overwhelming peace in my heart. I am no longer tormented by my past. I gave it to God, truly repented, asked for forgiveness, and the matter has been settled with God. I am *finally* at peace with myself. Praise God! My identity is in Christ, not my sexuality.

# 25. Hell Is Still a Burning Issue

Understandably, Hell is an uncomfortable subject. No one wants to believe such a place exists but if Jesus talked about Hell, shouldn't we? He spoke more on Hell than Heaven, signifying the importance of believing in such a place.

In Mark 9:43, 45, 47, Jesus said: "And if thy hand offend thee, cut it off: it is better for thee to enter into life maimed, than having two hands to go into Hell, into the fire that never shall be quenched." Jesus is making a point. Hell is no joke.

Jesus often spoke in parables, which were used to illustrate a truth in a way people could understand. Parables are not myths. They are earthly stories with a Heavenly meaning and a spiritual truth. The following parable is the only one in which Jesus used the names of real people: Lazarus, Abraham, and Moses. In this parable, Jesus portrays two destinies upon death: Heaven and Hell. "Physical death" is the separation of soul from the body, while "spiritual death" is the separation of the soul from God. Jesus warned we should be most concerned about spiritual death: "...fear Him which is able to destroy both soul and body in Hell" (Matthew 10:28).

19 "There was a certain rich man who was clothed in purple and fine linen and fared sumptuously every day. 20 But there was a certain beggar named Lazarus, full of sores, who was laid at his gate, 21 desiring to be fed with the crumbs which fell from the rich man's table. Moreover the dogs came and licked his sores. 22 So it was that the beggar died, and was carried by the angels to Abraham's bosom. The rich man also died and

was buried. 23 And being in torments in Hell, he lifted up his eyes and saw Abraham afar off, and Lazarus in his bosom.

24 Then he cried and said, 'Father Abraham, have mercy on me, and send Lazarus that he may dip the tip of his finger in water and cool my tongue; for I am tormented in this flame.' 25 But Abraham said, 'Son, remember that in your lifetime you received your good things, and likewise Lazarus evil things; but now he is comforted and you are tormented. 26 And besides all this, between us and you there is a great gulf fixed, so that those who want to pass from here to you cannot, nor can those from there pass to us.'

27 Then he said, 'I beg you therefore, father, that you would send him to my father's house, 28 for I have five brothers, that he may testify to them, lest they also come to this place of torment.' 29 Abraham said to him, 'They have Moses and the prophets; let them hear them.' 30 And he said, 'No, father Abraham; but if one goes to them from the dead, they will repent.' 31 But he said to him, 'If they do not hear Moses and the prophets, neither will they be persuaded though one rise from the dead'" (Luke 16:19-31).

In the beginning portion of Luke 16:1-18, Jesus addressed the religious leaders. They were concerned with outward appearances. Jesus was concerned with what was on the inside that could defile a person. It's the heart that matters. The religious leaders scoffed when Jesus accused them of being self-righteous and trying to earn their way into the Kingdom on their own terms. They refused to believe He was the Messiah. God's Word is silent about Lazarus' belief but somewhere in his life he had to have come to the knowledge that Jesus is who He claimed to be, and believed.

We can glean enough information from the parable of the rich man and Lazarus to know this much about Hell. The rich man has his memory. He not only remembers Lazarus but he also remembers his brothers and *pleads* with Abraham to have someone warn them about "this place of torment."  He can physically feel for he is in pain and torment from a flame.  He is also thirsty.  The rich man had everything life could offer and what did it gain him in the end?  Nothing!

Sadly, most preachers today refuse to acknowledge Hell for fear of offending or frightening people.  We, as Christians, are called to be soldiers for Christ:  unafraid, uncompromising, and unashamed in speaking the truth of God's Word.  All of it.

Hell was not created for us and God never intended for us to be there.  Jesus said that Hell was prepared for the devil and his angels (Matthew 25:41), and that in His Father's house are many mansions and that He goes to prepare a place for us (John 14:2).  Just as there is a literal Heaven, Jesus' literal blood was shed to save us from a literal Hell.  To contradict God is equivalent to calling Him a liar.  If there is no Hell for unrepentant sinners then there is no Hell for Satan and his angels.  God has already declared where they will spend eternity (Revelation 20:10).  The Lake of Fire will be the perpetual abode of Satan, his angels, and impenitent sinners who rejected God's plan of salvation.  Why would a loving God create such a horrific place?  Until we understand the intensity of God's love for us, only then can we understand the intensity of His judgment.  None of God's characteristics will be found in Hell.  It is the complete antithesis of Heaven.  Here is what we know about Hell, according to God's Word:

- Hell is a prison that houses every enemy of God.

- There is no light in Hell because God is light (1 John 1:5). Hell is described as "outer darkness" and flames (Matthew 8:12; 22:13; Revelation 16:10; Jude 1:13).

- God is life (John 1:4). Things we take for granted here on Earth such as the beauty of flowers, lush green meadows, and colorful leaves on trees in the fall season, are not found in Hell.

- The sounds of Hell. We are told it's a place of "weeping, wailing, and gnashing of teeth forever" (Matthew 13:42; 22:12-13; Luke 13:28). You won't hear birds singing, the soothing sound of rain, or the laughter of children in Hell.

- Because God is love (1 John 4:16), without the presence of God in Hell, no love will be found. You will never hear another individual tell you how much they love you.

- God is merciful (Psalm 36:5). Hell is void of any mercy. There will be horrific torment in Hell.

- There is no water in Hell. The rich man asked for only "one drop of water to cool his tongue" yet that request was denied (Luke 16:23-24).

- Jesus is the "prince of peace" (Isaiah 9:6). You will never have a moment's peace in Hell due to the torment and screams. You will never have a moment of silence.

- "...and they have no rest day nor night..." (Revelation 14:11). You don't even get to sleep in Hell.

- Hell is a fiery furnace where the fire is never quenched... meaning it will never go out (Matthew 13: 49-50; Mark 9:43-48). God's Word speaks of "fire and brimstone" (sulfur). It is said that the boiling point for sulfur (before turning from a liquid to a gas) is approximately 832 degrees Fahrenheit. This gives us some idea how hot Hell is. It is also said that the fumes from sulfur are "toxic and dangerously irritating" and that you will not be able to bear it as gives you a choking feeling. It will be hard to breathe in Hell.

- There is no hope in Hell. There is no exit door, no hope of ever escaping Hell (Matthew 25:46; Luke 16:25-26). God's eternal decree confirms there is a gulf that is "fixed" between an eternal Heaven and an everlasting Hell. Once you pass through the doorway of death without Christ, your fate is sealed.

- You will have your memory in Hell (Luke 16:27-28). Your conscience will torment you, living with the eternal regret of not heeding God's warning. You will live with the fact that God made a way for you to escape Hell but you refused to listen.

Where I spend eternity is my decision and I only have two choices. Jesus firmly declares that there is only one chance to escape Hell and that's *in this life*, before you die (John 5:24; John 3:16). In Luke 16:22-23, Jesus makes clear that when the rich man died he immediately went to a place of torment. Death is sudden and Hell is immediate.

I often hear people say, "God is loving and wouldn't allow people to suffer like that." Well six million Jews suffered and died at the hands of Hitler. Christians have been persecuted and murdered all over the world for centuries. God allowed His Son, Jesus, to suffer and be crucified. So what makes us think He won't allow suffering in Hell for unrepentant sinners who deliberately rejected Jesus?

God is dogmatic about the way you must come to Him. There is only one way to God and only one way to escape Hell and that's through Jesus. It grieves God to see souls going to Hell. God "takes no pleasure in the death of the wicked but that they repent and turn from their evil ways" (Ezekiel 33:11). He "...is patient with us, not wanting anyone to perish, but that everyone come to repentance" (2 Peter 3:9).

# 26. God's Plan For Your Life

If you do not know Jesus as your Savior, I encourage you to give your life to Christ. Christians aren't the enemy. The world does not care about you or where you spend eternity. God commands Christians to share the Gospel of Christ. The message may be hard to digest, and may not always be delivered in *love*, but there is nothing in *this* temporary world worth risking being eternally separated from God.

Scripture declares religion and good works will never save your soul. You can work yourself to death and you will still go to Hell. Religion does not have the power to make evil men holy. Many know *about* God but don't *know* God. Many pay lip service to God but have no respect for Him, or His laws, nor do they care about obeying Him. We can be faithful to a church and yet not be faithful to God.

There are people who are "religious" in name only and are going to Hell. It doesn't matter if you're Jew or Gentile. Jesus taught we must be "born again" (Romans 10:9-13). None of us can bypass Jesus. This doesn't mean being "sprinkled" as an infant. A baby is incapable of being convicted of sin and turning away from it. We must be of an age where we recognize our sinful nature and have the ability to make a conscious decision to willingly give our life to Christ. We cannot earn, take credit for, or buy *salvation*. This offer has been extended to us because of God's grace, not works. Grace and works are mutually exclusive (Romans 11:6).

God's free gift of salvation is offered to anyone who wants it *but the offer expires upon death.*

For those who pray to Mary (the mother of Jesus) or other saints, 1 Timothy 2:5 declares, "For there is one God, and one mediator between God and men, the man Christ Jesus." Jesus is the *only* mediator. Mary and other saints cannot mediate our prayer requests to God.

There is no such thing as reincarnation or a place called "purgatory." You cannot "pray a dead person into Heaven" even if they didn't accept Jesus as their Savior. God's Word does not support these lies. Once you die, your fate is sealed (Hebrews 9:27). If it were true that one could be prayed into Heaven after death, I would certainly live life as I pleased and then have people "pray me into Heaven" when I died. Only in this life do we have the opportunity to be reconciled to God. Trust God and take Him at His word. It is the shed blood of Jesus that makes us holy, sinless, and righteous in God's eyes (Matthew 26:28; Hebrews 10:19; 13:12; 1 John 1:7-9). We do not work to be *saved*. The Cross, where Jesus shed His blood, will either become *your salvation or your damnation. Your conscience* will either convict you or harden your heart. What we do with this message counts forever.

I have heard some people say they want nothing to do with God because of Christians. I certainly understand that attitude but the fallacy in that thinking is that it does not absolve us from our responsibility concerning our salvation. I could have taken the easy way out and said to God that I rejected Him because of my unfortunate experience with *some* Christians. However, I am an adult with the ability to reason. God declared that I am a sinner in need of salvation and *I had the choice* to either accept or reject this revelation. I will not be able to stand before God and blame others. God will hold me personally responsible for my decision. Every one of us shall given account of himself to God (Romans 14:12). The way of the Cross is the way to Heaven through Jesus.

When Jesus said, "It is finished!" it was not the shout of a victim, but a victor! He didn't say, "'I' am finished." He said, "'IT' is finished!" The Greek word for finished being *teleo* or "paid to the end of paying" meaning there's nothing else left to pay. The sin issue has been settled for all of eternity because of Jesus' shed blood (Hebrews Chapter 9; and 10:10-14).

Do you know how important you are to God? Jesus said: "I say unto you...joy shall be in Heaven...in the presence of the angels of God over one sinner that repents" (Luke 15:7&10). It doesn't matter what our sins are. God makes it clear, and promises, all sins will be forgiven if we come His way, and He promises to remember them no more (Isaiah 43:25; Hebrews 8:12; Psalm 103:12). There is no day, no hour, in which God is not ready to forgive the most grievous of sins from a truly repentant sinner.

Many people are hurting and unable to see how life can get any better but God *is* in the deliverance business. He *wants* to heal our wounds and set us free from bondage if we let Him. God did it for me, and He will do it for anyone who comes to Him and cries out for help. Satan wants to keep us in bondage but we are victorious in Christ!

If you are moved by what Jesus did on your behalf and would like to give your life to Christ and accept Him as your personal Savior, it's very simple. Just read the following scriptures. If you are in agreement, a sample prayer has been included at the end. You are choosing, by your own free will, to give your life to Christ. *You can change the eternal destination of your soul at this very moment*!

**God says in order to go to Heaven you must be born again:** This is not a physical rebirth, but a spiritual rebirth (John 3:7).

**You realize you are a sinner:** "For all have sinned, and come short of the glory of God; Being justified freely by His grace through the redemption that is in Christ Jesus" (Romans 3:23-24; 5:12; 1 John 1:8-10).

**Because you are a sinner, you are condemned to death:** "For the wages (payment) of sin is death; but the gift of God is eternal life through Jesus Christ our Lord" (Romans 6:23). This includes eternal separation from God. We are spiritual beings and will live for eternity. Where do you want to spend it?

**Jesus had to shed His blood and die:** "But God commends His love toward us, in that, while we were yet sinners, Christ died for us. Much more then, being now justified by His blood, we shall be saved from wrath through Him" (Romans 5:8-9; Romans 4:25; 1 Peter 3:18).

**Repent and turn from sin:** Jesus said: "I tell you, Nay: but, except you repent, you shall all likewise perish" (Luke 13:3; Acts 2:38; 17:30). The Greek word for repent being "Metanoia" means to turn to someone or something from someone or something. Turn to Christ from sin.

**You believe in Jesus:** "For God so loved the world, that He gave His only begotten Son, that whosoever believes in Him should not perish, but have everlasting life. For God sent not

His Son into the world to condemn the world; but that the world through Him might be saved. He that believes on Him is not condemned: but he that believes not is condemned already, because he hath not believed in the name of the only begotten Son of God." (John 3:16-18) "All that the Father gives Me shall come to Me; and him that come to Me I will in no wise cast out." (John 6:37) No one, including you, will be turned away.

**You confess with your mouth that Jesus is Lord and believe in the finished work of what Jesus did on the Cross:** "Wherefore God also hath highly exalted him, and given him a name which is above every name: That at the name of Jesus every knee should bow, of things in Heaven, and things in earth, and things under the earth; And that every tongue should confess that Jesus Christ is Lord, to the glory of God the Father." (Philippians 2:9-11; also Romans 14:11-12) "Whosoever shall confess that Jesus is the Son of God, God dwells in him, and he in God." (1 John 4:15; Romans 10:9)

**You want to receive Jesus?** "...what must I do to be saved...Believe on the Lord Jesus Christ, and thou shall be saved..." (Acts 16:30-31; Romans 10:10 & 13; John 1:12). This doesn't mean "maybe." It is a guaranteed fact.

This decision is not about the religion of Christianity. It is about a personal relationship with God. Truly desire to know Him. This is strictly between you and God. Salvation must be viewed from God's perspective. God can't make you accept Jesus as your Savior and Satan can't keep you from coming to Christ.

One of the unalterable truths that each individual must learn is that we cannot bypass Jesus to get to God. We cannot reject Jesus Christ as Savior and Lord and approach the throne of grace and expect Almighty God to answer our prayers. Jesus taught we are to pray in His name and God will hear it because we are praying with His authority and asking God to answer our prayers according to His will (John 14:13-14; 1 John 5:14-15).

Note that saying this prayer doesn't guarantee salvation if you're just saying this prayer as "fire insurance" against Hell. God knows the heart, and your motive. Do not go to Him in a deceitful manner because you will be wasting your time. You must sincerely mean it with all your heart. If you're in agreement with what you've read, and wish to give your life to Christ, simply pray:

> *"Heavenly Father, I come before you and confess that I am a sinner and have sinned against you. I'm asking for your forgiveness. I believe that Christ died for my sins, was buried and rose again, as the Scripture teaches. It is written in Your Word that if I confess with my mouth that Jesus is Lord and believe in my heart that you raised Him from the dead, I shall be saved. Right now I choose to receive Christ as my Savior. I confess that Jesus is Lord. I renounce my past life with Satan and close the door to any of his devices. Thank you for forgiving me of all my sin. Father God, take my life and give me the strength to live for You. In Jesus name I pray. Amen."*

If you prayed this prayer with all sincerity, congratulations, and welcome to the family of God! Here are a few things you can do to help you grow spiritually.

Find a Bible-believing church (Hebrews 10:25). If you are unsure of a church, most websites will list their "doctrinal statement" or you can request one from the church.

Beware of any pastor, individual, or church that doesn't believe the Bible is the infallible Word of God, written under the inspiration of the Holy Spirit. Beware of anyone who will not confess with his or her mouth that Jesus is Lord. Beware of anyone who teaches there are many paths to God, that we are all good, that you can work to earn your salvation, that everyone goes to Heaven, that Jesus is *not* God's Son, and denies the existence of a literal Hell. Beware of anyone who denies the Virgin Birth, Vicarious Sacrifice, Victorious Resurrection, and impending return of Jesus (the Rapture). These are just a few examples of how quickly to spot a wolf in sheep's clothing. Once you find a Bible-believing church, speak with a pastor about your decision for Christ and that you want to be baptized. This is in obedience to the Lord Jesus Christ as a public testimony of your salvation.

Read the Bible daily (2 Timothy 2:15) for this is how God talks to you. Try reading a few chapters every day. Before reading, pray and ask God to give you the wisdom to help you understand His Word (James 1:5-6).

Pray continually to God about everything that is on your heart. Pray for friends and family. Praise Him and thank Him for your blessings (1 Thessalonians 5:17).

Witness. Share what Christ has done for you, especially with your family and friends (Mark 5:19). You do not want your loved ones suffering in Hell.

Develop relationships with people who can help you spiritually. If there are people who try to pull you back into your old life, sever ties with them. You will lose most of your "worldly" friends but God will put the right kind of people in your life.

When you are feeling troubled, pray to God and keep Christ-centered gospel music playing in the background. Demons cannot stand to hear the name of Jesus. Find music that is soft, simple, and keeps your mind completely focused on Jesus.

"These things I have spoken unto you, that in Me you might have peace. In the world you shall have tribulation: but be of good cheer; I have overcome the world" (John 16:33). "Yea, though I walk through the valley of the shadow of death, I will fear no evil: for thou art with me; thy rod and thy staff they comfort me" (Psalm 23:4).

"Peace I leave with you, my peace I give unto you: not as the world gives, give I unto you. Let not your heart be troubled, neither let it be afraid" (John 14:27). "And the peace of God, which passes all understanding, shall keep your hearts and minds through Christ Jesus" (Philippians 4:7).

# 27. Knockin' on Heaven's Door

God doesn't say a lot about Heaven. Quite honestly, I don't think words can do it justice. But we are told this much...Heaven is real. God created it (Genesis 1:1-8; John 14:1-3). Jesus sits at the right hand of God in Heaven (Psalm 110:1; Luke 22:69; 1 Peter 3:22).

John, the author of the book of Revelation, was allowed a glimpse into Heaven and gives a beautiful description of it in Revelation 21:10-27; 22:1-5; and 7:17. I encourage you to read it for yourself.

"The grace of our Lord Jesus Christ be with you all. Amen." (Revelation 22:21).

## To God be the glory.

For permission requests, media interviews,
or general information, please visit:
https://www.georgecarneal.com
https://youtube.com/c/georgecarneal/videos
https://rumble.com/c/georgecarneal
https://www.bitchute.com/channel/georgecarneal/
https://www.brighteon.com/channels/georgecarneal

Made in the USA
Coppell, TX
08 October 2021